T

How
small
groups
can raise
BIG
FUNDS

How
small
groups
can raise
BIG
FUNDS

Editor: Roni Jay

new tricks for old dogs

Published by White Ladder Press Ltd
Great Ambrook, Near Ipplepen, Devon TQ12 5UL
01803 813343
www.whiteladderpress.com

First published in Great Britain in 2007

10 9 8 7 6 5 4 3 2 1

Designed and typeset by Julie Martin Ltd
Cover design by Julie Martin Ltd
Cover photograph by Jonathon Bosley
Cover printed by St Austell Printing Company
Printed and bound by TJ International Ltd, Padstow, Cornwall

Printed on totally chlorine-free paper
The paper used for the text pages of this book is FSC certified.
FSC (The Forest Stewardship Council) is an international
network to promote responsible management of the world's forests.

FSC
Mixed Sources
Product group from well-managed
forests and other controlled sources
Cert no. SGS-COC-2482
www.fsc.org
© 1996 Forest Stewardship Council

 White Ladder books are distributed in the UK by Virgin Books

White Ladder Press
Great Ambrook, Near Ipplepen, Devon TQ12 5UL
01803 813343
www.whiteladderpress.com

Contents

Acknowledgements

Elaine Aronson, Suzy Baker, Nicky Bell, Richard Birch, Antonia Bolingbroke-Kent, Larry Boyd, David Butler, Becky Coleman, Lizzy Cornelius, Dave Cornthwaite, Jo Crocker, Simon Doggett, Mohinder Dosanjh, Ray Edensor, Natasha Evans, Ben Ewan, Josette Falzon, Ben Fillmore, London Fitness, Sarah Foster, UK Fundraising, Michael Garry, Steven Hardaker, Kerry Hayes, Pauline Hedges, Dave Heeley, Susan Hill, Jane Hopkins, The Celebrity Index, Mair James, Sandre Jones, Justgiving, Howard Lake, Becky Magson, Time Outdoors, Claire Park, The Red Pages, Tony Poderis, Jennifer Rivers, Dale Russell, Kitty Shiner, Jason Slack, Sam Spreadbury, Elizabeth Thompson, John Thompson, Nina Tsang, Steven Watts, Martin Whittle, Julia Williams, Emma Wykes.

Introduction

Fundraising – everyone's at it. Whether you're planning on running a marathon or jumping out of a plane in aid of a charity that's close to your heart, holding a series of coffee mornings to raise enough money to buy a much-needed new wheelchair for a disabled child, or organising a large-scale black tie ball to pay for urgent repairs to the church roof, if you've picked up this book then you're likely to be one of the many thousands of people planning fundraising efforts right now.

This means that competition for the money that people are willing to give is extremely tough. Most of us have pet charities and causes that we support already. On top of those come the requests from friends, family and colleagues undertaking a sponsored challenge or fundraising event. And on top of *that*, there are the community events that you feel you should support, such as a village fête or show. That's just on a small, individual level – imagine how many times a week businesses and celebrities are asked to donate money, their time, or their endorsement.

When you enter the fundraising arena you're also entering into competition with the professional fundraisers who work for charities and who have experience and knowledge of marketing and event-planning that you may not have. As such they already have an edge.

So how can you, as an individual or a small group, make sure that you start from a strong position, stand out from the clamouring crowd and get your slice of the pie?

Charity fundraiser Ray Edensor, known as 'The Running Paramedic', uses the following five-point plan.

- **Belief.** You must believe in the charity you are raising money for. Get as much information as possible about the work the charity does and how it goes about it. Find something personal to you, that you care about.

- **Plan.** Sit down and draw up a plan of action. Decide how much you're going to raise. Look at newspapers and magazines for stories of how other people have raised money and then go one better.

- **Highs and lows.** The highs will come when your target is getting closer; the lows come when you have taken hours and hours planning an event and the response is poor. If this happens, don't give up, because the next event may well be a success.

- **Media.** The media like to report on someone who is doing something different, and it is sometimes the media coverage that helps bring in the sponsors.

- **Enjoy.** Lastly you must get pleasure from raising the money, so think of events that you and your friends are going to enjoy.

There are some recurring themes throughout this book – messages that cropped up again and again while I was picking the brains of the people who generously gave their time to share their experiences. You'll notice them yourself if you read the book straight through, but as you may prefer to dip in and out, I want to pick up on them here as well and bring them to the forefront.

Plan, plan, plan

There is no substitute for really thorough, detailed planning. Make sure you leave plenty of time – rushing things through is a recipe for half-baked planning, things getting forgotten or not thought through properly, and an event that flops rather than fizzes.

Your planning should involve things like:

- Keeping a master checklist of everything that needs to be done, when by and keeping it updated.

- Setting a target amount of money to be raised. This might be decided already by your aim (for example, the cost of a piece of equipment), or it might be an amount that you decide upon as being realistic to raise with a certain kind of event to give to a charity. Either way, make sure the amount is achievable within the time you have available.

> **Top tip** £££££££££££££££££££££££££££££££
>
> It's important to set yourself a target. It should be one that you think you can reach so as not to disappoint yourself by setting one that's way too high and not reaching it. *Josette Falzon, fundraiser for the Cystic Fibrosis Trust*

- Having a schedule. A wall calendar is a good way of seeing at a glance whether you are on track.

- Having a budget. Fundraising can cost money at the start. Where is this money going to come from? And make sure you don't overspend, eating into your profits.

- Double-checking everything. For example, make sure your figures are right, make sure your planned date doesn't clash with any major events that will mean fewer people will turn up, make sure all details are correct on promotional materials before they go to press.

Top tip £££££££££££££££££££££££££££££££££

The Bollywood night we organised was not very well attended. The reasons for it being unpopular were that we organised it at short notice and we did not have enough time to promote it. *Mohinder Dosanjh, of the Trinjan Women's Social and Community Group, London*

Use your imagination

When thinking of ideas for ways you can raise money, thinking about how you can publicise your events, or thinking of lists of people to ask for help, the more imaginative and creative you are the more likely you will be to come up with fresh, exciting ideas that get people inspired and raise both money and awareness. In such a competitive field you must stand out from the crowd if you are to succeed, and the way to do that is to do something new, something fun. Let your imagination run wild!

BRIGHT IDEA

Our fundraisers are very innovative and creative. People enjoy participating in them. Normally we get in touch with people on members' recommendations. For example we needed a trainer to train our participants for a fashion show. Someone recommended a Bollywood dance coach who trained people for modelling for our fundraiser. He gave his services free because it was a good promotion for his business. People with no formal training in modelling loved doing it because they had the opportunity to dress up in very elegant dresses. It was something different. Mohinder Dosanjh

Think links

This idea of links came up over and over again when I was talking to successful fundraisers.

Think links when:

- Thinking of ideas for events – how does a barbecue link to an eye hospital, for example? Would it be better to hold a sponsored silly sunglasses day, or spend a day blindfold?

- Asking for celebrities to get involved – what's the link; why would they want to support *your* cause?

- Asking businesses to donate prizes or give services for free – is there a link between them and your cause? Find one.

- Coming up with ideas for publicising your event – how could local and national media link your event into a news story or feature?

- What sort of food are you going to serve at your event, if any? Does it link to the idea for the event, or the charity, for example?

- What fancy dress should you wear to do your sponsored walk? Make it link back to your cause, so it stands out and sticks in people's minds.

Be professional

Treat your fundraising efforts like a small business. This means keeping records, being professional in your approach to people, being polite. Network in the same way as you would if this was your job. If you meet someone who might be able and willing to help you, make a note of their contact details, and follow up the encounter with a phone call or email a few days later.

Part of being professional is *doing your research*. No businessperson would start a new venture without thoroughly researching their market first – and you should apply the same principles to fundraising ventures. You're trying to make money as well; the fact that it is going to be donated to others doesn't change that. So make sure that the market exists for your product, or that the community can sustain the sort of event you are planning, or that you will be able to sell enough tickets to make it viable, before you commit to anything.

Don't assume anything

Especially not that anyone will give you their time, money or goods simply because 'it's for charity'. It just isn't enough. So always think – what's in it for them?

- When it comes to selling your product or event, you need to think what you are offering people. A great day out? A unique product? What's your 'unique selling point'?

- When approaching businesses or other potential sponsors – offer them something in return. Whether that's advertising, the chance to meet a celebrity, or something else – the important thing is that you don't expect to get something for nothing.

Pack it out

Don't just hold a coffee morning – include a competition, or game or recipe swap as well. If you're organising an auction, think about turning it into a dinner, or selling tickets to a disco afterwards as well. Sell refreshments at a duck race. Whatever it is that you are doing, make sure you maximise the fundraising potential within your event.

Be passionate

Nothing will sell your cause like real passion for it and dedication to it. So if you're undertaking a sponsored event and are in the process of looking for something to support, pick something you really care about. The most successful fundraisers are often those who are raising money for something very close to their heart, simply because their feeling and enthusiasm are infectious. Take a tip from them and let everyone know just how much this campaign deserves their cash. Fundraising can be a hard slog at times and you may have to knock on a lot of doors before you are successful. This is where passion and dedication will keep you going.

Top tip £££££££££££££££££££££££££££££££

It's extremely important that you are dedicated to what you are doing. You have to keep in mind that you do not get a penny out of this but then again satisfaction is more important. Also, you have to be prepared that not every fundraising event might be successful – but never ever to give up. When people know that it's all for a very worthy cause, they will definitely help. *Josette Falzon*

Be direct, be specific

When you're asking for something, ask directly. Fudging and hedging around the issue will just annoy people. And be specific – asking for 'help' or 'support' is too fuzzy and people are likely to turn down your request simply because they are unsure of what exactly is being asked of them. Instead, ask for a specific item, attendance at a dinner, or a set amount of money.

BRIGHT IDEA

Don't be afraid to ask for money. We raised almost half of our total so far from a direct appeal to the Church community – everyone gave what they felt able to, ranging from a few hundred pounds to thousands. *Sam Spreadbury, treasurer, Bassingbourn Church Appeal*

Publicity, promotion and the press

This should be right at the top of your list of priorities. Use every method at your disposal – telephone, letters, email, the internet, word of mouth, flyers, posters – there are so many ways you can get your message out there, but the more creative you can be the better. Proof-read everything. Use images to create eye-catching posters and flyers. Make sure your writing is clear, concise, and snappy. Spread the net as wide as you possibly can and you'll be more likely to reap the rewards.

If you're unsure, make sure

Particularly when it comes to safety, insurance, licences, permissions, regulations . . . if in doubt, your local council is usually the first port of call regarding anything official like this.

And finally – always, always, remember to say thank you.

How to use this book

The first part of the book is an ideas bank containing hundreds of different ways to raise money. It includes some old favourites (as well some ideas on how to give them a fresh twist), some new ideas, and some contributions from inspiring individuals and small groups who have successfully raised big money. It doesn't attempt to be comprehensive but provides you with lots of starting points for your own ideas, practical advice, top tips and things to watch out for, as well as the real-life experiences of those who have gone before you, for you to learn from.

The second part deals with some of the specifics of planning and organising a fundraising event. It is broken down into five sections – *Planning; Celebrities; Businesses and sponsors; Publicity and media; Rules and regulations.* As with the *Ideas* section, this part of the book contains tips from experienced fundraisers.

Part 1

Ideas for events

Community events

The only thing that really limits what you can do to raise money is your imagination. What follows here should provide you with lots of ideas to get started, but some of the most successful events are the most personal, the ones that come from you, or the cause you are fundraising for. As suggested in the introduction – think links! Is there a venue in your area that would make a fabulous setting for a sale or dinner? Does your charity have an image, logo, or particular feature that might spark your imagination? Is there a local business, personality or attraction that could be used as the central part of a fundraising event? These are the elements that will personalise your event, and increase the amount of money you can make. But if you're stuck, this section includes hundreds of tried and tested ideas, as well as some new ones that you can take and adapt to suit you.

Talks, tours and trips

Talks from any local experts, on anything from gardening to Groucho Marx.

Restoration and renovation projects lend themselves well to talks by experts about the history of the buildings in question, and the local architecture and history in general.

Open gardens give a chance for keen gardeners to show off their displays. Some people like to provide teas and sell plants and flowers in their gardens as part of an open day.

Boat trips or **days out** to stately homes, museums or other places of interest.

Treasure hunt. Research your local history and construct a set of clues that take people around some of the area's landmarks – think churches, town halls, old cinemas, village greens. Charge people to take part in a treasure hunt.

Tour of local churches would be appropriate for church fundraising, as would **talks** on church history and **sponsor** a slate. This is a solid way of raising money within a community. Think about giving donors who sponsor a slate a certificate, or listing their names somewhere public as a way of saying thanks.

Top tip ££££££££££££££££££££££££££££££££££

Run events which can engage everyone. Our most successful event was a Bible Reading Marathon where the whole Bible was read non-stop in ten-minute slots over three days and three nights. We had an amazing amount of support from the wider village (certainly not just the usual suspects) because it was really different, and everyone could get involved. As well as drawing in the financial support we were seeking, it also really raised the profile of the church in the village. So you'll often find that you get two benefits in tandem. *Sam Spreadbury*

Concerts

Musical evenings of all kinds are consistently popular. Many communities will have an orchestra, amateur operatic society, choir or rock group who will be keen to get involved and show off their collective talents, especially if it's in aid of a local good cause.

Gigs can also be a great thing for schools and teenagers to organise – and arc far cooler than a cake sale.

Ideas for concerts:

- Organ recital
- Gospel choir
- Children's concert
- Christmas carol concert
- Jazz concert
- Rock concert
- Jazz and blues night
- Open mic night

Fashion show

A fashion show is a good way for local businesses to get involved in fundraising as they can also benefit from the exposure. Contact your local art or design college as fashion students may well be willing to offer their skills helping out – dressing, coaching and finding suitable models, for example – in return for some of their designs being showcased.

Remember it's not haute couture – display a wide range of clothes suitable for all shapes, sizes and ages, so that there's something for everyone.

Beauty contest

A Miss World-style contest, or a spoof one.

BRIGHT IDEA ☀

We raise a lot of money every year with our drag beauty contest, called Miss Lyneham. There's a swimwear category, evening wear, a talent spot, and they give a little speech on why they should be Miss Lyneham. All of the profits go to charity, including those from the bar for the night. *Kerry Hayes, RAF Lyneham*

Sports and races

Race night. Films of horse (or other animal) races are shown and the organiser runs a tote, taking bets on who will win. There are lots of companies who will either run the whole night for you, or provide DIY Race Night Packs with full instructions – look in the Yellow Pages or do an internet search for one near you.

Greyhound racing. Most of the greyhound racing stadiums will help you to organise a race evening for charity. See the section on *Grand events* for tips on organising a larger night out such as this.

Duck race. Bulk-buy plastic ducks and number them with a permanent marker (make sure it's waterproof). You'll need to find a stretch of river that is fast-flowing enough to get the race going, and still shallow enough for the ducks to be easily collected at the end of the race. You'll also need to be able to section off the end-point somehow, with netting or a barrier. Remember to get permission from the landowner before making any further plans. Money is raised through the 'sale' of the ducks (give people a raffle ticket with their corresponding number when they buy their ducks) and through any supplementary activities such as stalls or food and drink sales.

Snail race. It's never going to be a fast-paced race, but snail races can provide plenty of slow-burning excitement, and make a fun focal point for a fundraising day.

Golf tournament. Teams of golfers buy tickets to the tournament, which can include lunch or dinner in the price.

BRIGHT IDEA

How about holding an auction or raffle of golf-related memorabilia and prizes at the event?

Matches. Five-a-side football, cricket, rounders – whatever the sport, getting people's competitive streak going makes for an exciting and enjoyable day, with lots of opportunities for side-events to raise money.

CASE STUDY

'Blind Dave' Heeley has raised an amazing £150,000-plus from various fundraising events, including a celebrity cricket match. He's now aiming to become the first disabled athlete to run seven marathons in seven days on seven continents, a feat previously achieved by only two people, Sir Ranulph Fiennes and Dr Mike Stroud, who ran together.

Dave had the idea of organising a celebrity cricket match in 2004 when he heard a radio interview with David English, founder and organiser of Bunbury's, the celebrity cricket team. He contacted David and explained that the 75th anniversary of Guide Dogs for the Blind was coming up and he would like Bunbury's to be involved. David readily agreed and put together a team. The day raised thousands of pounds for Dave's chosen charity.

Top tips £££££££££££££££££££££££££££££

Dave's recommendations for organising a charity sports match are:

- Check dates don't coincide with other major events nationally or locally, such as the FA Cup final.

- Be persistent, don't give up, the door will open at some time.

- When it comes to getting publicity, phone anyone and everyone, just basically be a nuisance.

- Sell your tickets well before the game.

- An auction is a good way of raising more money on the day, as is asking companies to sponsor tables.

Themed events

Game shows. Hold your own version of a TV game show. This could either be a quiz-based show or a more active one. It's a great way of organising a day of fun activities for all the family, or a more adult-orientated night event.

Blind Date. Particularly popular with students, have someone play Cilla and, if possible, someone backstage being the voice of the ever-popular 'Our Graham'.

CASE STUDY

Ben Ewan, Cambridge University's 2006-07 RAG president, says: "The most successful event we run is Blind Date, which raises approximately £10,000 each year. It has slowly built up to become a cult classic among Cambridge students. It's a simple idea but isn't taken too seriously and seems to work well with students.

"We sell forms for £5 which have promotional offers on the back for the night. Then the girls and boys fill out their forms and send them back to their college reps. We have a massive swap when all the college reps do their best to swap people who are compatible, but it inevitably becomes a bit of a free for all."

Bullseye. Get your local pub darts players together for a Bullseye themed night.

Call My Bluff. Two teams of three players compete against each other, taking it in turns to provide three definitions of an unusual word, only one of which is right. The opposing team then has to guess who is bluffing, and whose definition is the correct one.

Catchphrase. Draw or use Clip Art to put together images that represent familiar catchphrases, and have contestants ring a bell or call out when they think they know the answer.

Countdown. The 'letters rounds' are the ones that are best suited to community events. Get people anagram solving and making the longest words they can from a group of letters.

Have I Got News For You. Rounds in this current affairs quiz that could be adapted include a headline round, where contestants identify the news story associated with tabloid headlines, and the odd one out round, where contestants are shown four pictures of people or things and asked to identify the odd one out.

It's a Knockout. A great summer idea. You could hold a scaled-down version of this at a fête, or combine it with a spit roast or barbecue.

They Think It's All Over. This show contains all sorts of games. Ones which are easily adaptable include rounds where teams have to decide who said a sporting quote, and a 'name game' round where one member of the team is given the names of famous sportspeople and has to indicate the person by either describing them, drawing clues for their team-mates to guess from, or performing charades-style mimes.

Mastermind. Ask people who want to enter this to nominate their specialist subject in advance. You could hold early heats to decide who takes part in the eventual Mastermind evening and is named Village Mastermind, for example. Of course, you'll need a black swivel chair.

Never Mind the Buzzcocks. The TV pop music quiz show has a round where one team member must guess the song their team-mates are performing without using lyrics or instruments, which has great comic potential. Make sure you don't choose songs that are too obscure or too difficult to perform.

Through the Keyhole. You could have lots of fun making your own version of this show if you live in a small community where lots of people know each other and you can acquire the services of someone with a video camera.

Pop Idol or X-Factor. Find the star of your school or village with a singing competition—but beware the tongue-lashing from 'Simon Cowell'.

Whose Line is it Anyway? This improvisation-based show uses comedians on TV, but could work well for an amateur dramatics or theatre group as you do need confident performers for this to work. In the helping hands round, scenes are acted out by participants who are paired up, with one standing behind the other being their hands. In another, players have to make up a song in a style nominated by audience members.

BRIGHT IDEA ⚬

Think about linking the theme of the quiz to what you're trying to raise funds for. You could serve popcorn at a film quiz, and get film and TV related prizes for the winners.

Eurovision Song Contest. Host your own version of this classic talent show by allotting countries and songs to teams, and putting together a judging panel. Who will score the dreaded 'nul points'?

Quiz night. Pub-style quizzes are always fun. Get people to form teams and pay to enter. Also think about theming the questions.

Put together a gourmet hamper for the triumphant team in a food and drink quiz, and give tickets to a football match to the victors of a sports quiz.

Themed quiz ideas:

- Art
- Books
- An era – the Roaring Twenties or Swinging Sixties
- Films
- Food and drink
- Pop music
- Sports

BRIGHT IDEA

Compile a different quiz every month and sell the quiz sheets for a small amount within your community. Offer a prize for the most correct answers. Fundraising like this takes much less organisation than holding a public event and although it won't raise a huge amount of money, can provide a steady trickle of much-needed income.

Games

Beetle drives, bingo nights and whist drives are all popular, especially with older people.

Card games. Set up small 'stations' with tables and chairs at each one. Each table is for a different type of card game, but don't choose any that are too complicated. Some that work well are:

- Snap
- 21
- Rummy
- Whist
- Beggar-my-neighbour

Put an experienced player in charge of each game station and people can work their way around the room.

Board games. Perfect for a village hall or community centre, you provide as many board games as you can gather and people can bring their own as well. They pay an entrance fee which can either include the price of a buffet meal, or you can provide food for them to buy on the night.

Scrabble and Monopoly tournaments are great fun. Pick-Up Sticks and Jenga are something everyone can play and enjoy.

School disco. Go back to school in short trousers and long socks. This works best with a group of guests of similar ages so you can relive the 'best years of your life' through the music you all remember. For food, how about cones of chips, spotted dick and a tuck shop?

Pub games. Hold a traditional pub games night either in your local pub or in a hall or other room. Charge an entrance fee and include refreshments in the price – real ale and pies would be the perfect accompaniment to a night of bar skittles, shut the box, draughts, cribbage, Chinese checkers and Captain's Mistress.

Comedy night. Stand-up comedians at the beginning of their careers can often be booked for little or no fee, or, if you're organising a larger event you can try and get a bigger name star to perform.

Casino night. Roulette, poker and blackjack can all be played with Monopoly money, and a casino night can be a good excuse for everyone to get a bit glammed up. Make the dress code black tie, provide canapés and a cocktail or glass of fizz in the ticket price, and let the games begin!

Guinness Book of Records night. Compile a list of records people can attempt on the night from the book. Choose a good spread of different things so that there's something for everyone, and make sure you pick things that are safe and don't require too much special equipment.

Remote controlled cars day. This is an ideal event to hold in a school car park at the weekend. Get everyone to bring their remote-controlled vehicles along, charge an entrance fee and set up obstacle courses and races.

Pudding evening. Ideal for holding in the village hall, people eat dinner at home then come along for pudding afterwards. Make sure you have a good variety of puddings. You could even add an element of competition by getting people to vote for their favourite.

Cheese and wine evening. An oldie but still a goodie. Make sure this isn't just a bit of tired Cheddar and a glass of Chardonnay, but provide a well thought out selection of cheeses and complementary wines. Aim to have a good variety of cheese. Berry Bros and Rudd have a guide to matching cheese to wines on their website, at www.bbr.com, and any good cheese shop should also be able to guide you. Or consider hiring a wine expert from a company like Thirty Fifty, who run charity wine tastings [www.thirtyfifty.co.uk].

BRIGHT IDEA

Combine a wine tasting with an auction of wines and wine-related items.

Photo evening. Ask a local photographer to judge entrants' pictures in different categories, such as Best Family Photo, Best Holiday Photo, Best Baby Photo, Best Animal Photo, Best Nature Photo and Best Landscape. Hold a viewing evening at which the winners are announced. Ask businesses to donate items for prizes and provide refreshments for a charge.

Teddy bears' picnic. Go on a walk through the woods with a picnic of honey sandwiches and bear-shaped biscuits.

Country and Western evening. Hire a country band or a line dance caller. Rustle up a barbecue, ask a farmer to provide some straw bales, and get people to come dressed up for a hoedown. Present the best-dressed cowboy or girl with a prize.

1960s or 1970s evening. 'Era' themed evenings provide lots of opportunities to get creative with nostalgic decorations, food and fancy dress. A Sixties party is a great excuse for a disco with all your favourite Beatles and Motown tunes, while 'the decade that taste forgot' is always popular with fancy dress fans who love dressing up in flares, platform boots and afro wigs. How about including a quiz based on the decade's events? You could pin up pictures of celebrities from the era and get people to name them. Or display adverts from the time and see who can remember the slogans used alongside them.

Dinner party. If you're a keen cook, think about hosting a dinner party and charging friends to attend.

Themed dinner party ideas:

- **Italian evening.** Pizza, pasta, ciabatta bread, and round it off with tiramisu or zabaglione.

- **Retro recipes revival.** Prawn cocktail, steak Diane and black forest gateau.

- **Curry banquet.**

- **Fondue party.**

- **Celebrity chef.** All courses made using recipes from a particular celebrity chef, such as Jamie Oliver, Nigella Lawson, Gordon Ramsay or Hugh Fearnley-Whittingstall.

- **Chilli lovers.**

- **Cocktails and canapés**

- **American Diner.** Coke floats, burgers and key lime pie.

- **Fish and chips.** Perfect if you don't want to be chained to the kitchen as this doesn't require any cooking on the part of the host. Up the fun and sophistication by serving champagne or sparkling wine with your fish suppers.

Mad Hatter's tea party. An afternoon tea party with a difference – get everyone to come wearing their best or their silliest hat.

Chocoholics' morning. Gather everyone together for a chocolate themed version of the normal coffee morning. Chocolate fudge, brownies, truffles, biscuits and cakes are easy to make and then sell at stands on the day. Have a mug of hot chocolate instead of the usual tea and coffee. Set up a 'recipe swap' where people bring along their favourite chocolate recipes and pay a small amount to swap them with others. A chocoholics' tombola and raffle is fun and easy to put together – seek out things like chocolate liqueurs, candles and toiletries as well as the usual bars and boxes of chocolate. You could even hire a chocolate fountain. A local patisserie, chef or chocolate shop might agree to demonstrate techniques for cooking with chocolate.

Rock 'n' roll evening. Put on your blue suede shoes and maybe hire an Elvis or Shakin' Stevens look-a-like to really get everyone jiving.

Movie meal night. Contact your local cinema to discuss how you can organise a screening of a film in aid of your cause. Try and select a film that reflects what you are trying to raise money for, as well as including refreshments in the ticket price. On a smaller level, hold a movie night with your friends and family at home. Show *The Italian Job* and serve up slices of pizza, or caviar and blinis at a *Doctor Zhivago* night.

Australian night. Cork hats, sausages on the BBQ, and plenty of cold beer.

Pampering evening. Turn a hall or your living room into a spa for the night with a hired beauty therapist, or a local salon may donate their services for a reduced price. Manicures, mini-facials and make-up lessons are all ideally suited to a girly evening.

Murder mystery evening. These work especially well in stately homes or castles. Get inspiration for your tale of bloody murder from Agatha Christie stories, or there are kits you can buy with pre-written scripts.

Mexican night. Fajitas, piñatas, guacamole, margaritas, sombreros – a Mexican theme has lots of scope for a fantastic fiesta.

Catering for events

Some sorts of events might require you to comply with official food safety and hygiene legislation. When planning any event that involves serving food to members of the public it's best to contact the environmental health department at your local authority to find out whether you will be required to do this, and get their guidelines on food safety.

Below are some basic food safety tips. Find out more on the Food Standards Agency's website: www.eatwell.gov.uk

Labelling. If you're selling food, but not as part of a business (for a one-off charity event, for example), you probably won't be legally required to comply with the Food Labelling regulations. However, as with everything, it's always best to check with your local authority, which will be able to clarify things for you. If you're going to be selling food regularly – for example packs of home-made biscuits – you may have to comply with these regulations, even if you're not planning on keeping any profits. It is important that you make sure you know exactly where you stand.

Preparation. Be sure all surfaces and utensils (including your hands) are clean before you start cooking.

Don't use raw eggs in icings or anything that won't be completely cooked through.

Store any cakes that contain cream or butter icing well-refrigerated.

Store everything in clean, sealable containers, away from other foods. Be particularly careful with raw meat.

On the day. Make sure any cakes that need refrigeration (see above) aren't left out of the fridge for any longer than absolutely necessary. In fact, don't leave any foods out of the fridge for longer than you have to.

Use tongs or a cake slice when serving and handling cakes.

Make sure chilled foods are kept cold enough (at or below 8°C), and hot foods are kept hot enough (at or above 63°C).

When serving food, it can exceed or fall below these limits for a short period of time – up to four hours for chilled foods, and up to two hours for hot foods. After this, however, they must be disposed of – you can't reheat or chill foods repeatedly.

Sponsored events

Sponsored events – sporting or otherwise – are among the

first things that come to mind when people think of fundraising. There tend to be two approaches: it may be the challenge of taking part in a physically arduous event, such as the London Marathon, or it may be the pursuit and achievement of a personal goal, such as giving up smoking. Either way can be a good means of raising money.

If you already know what it is you want to undertake but are looking for a cause to raise money for, think carefully about who you will support. The advice from experienced fundraisers is that you need to feel some personal connection with your cause and you must be passionate about it if you are to raise lots of money. So think of what really matters to you – the issues and problems that you feel strongest about – then look for a charity or fund that has those aims.

Consider supporting a small, local charity, rather than one of the enormous and obvious choices. They do great work, but, especially in the case of a major marathon, will have hundreds if not thousands of people supporting them already. By choosing a smaller charity you have the opportunity to make a real difference and get involved in something where you can see exactly how the money you raise is changing people's lives for the better. And that's *real* satisfaction.

Alternatively, of course, plenty of sponsored runners, jumpers and walkers take part in these events as part of a larger programme of fundraising. If you are one of them this section should offer you plenty of ideas for events that might appeal to you, as well as tips on maximising the money you raise through them.

Marathons

Many people, be they beginners or experienced runners, choose to take part in a marathon to raise money for charity. In 2006, the average amount raised through each Justgiving.com website fundraising page for the London Marathon was £1,162.

It provides great motivation if you're trying to get fitter, a huge personal challenge and the opportunity to take part in a big event that can be really memorable and lots of fun.

If you've decided to take part in one, your next decision is which marathon it should be. London, Berlin, Paris, New York? Do you want one close to home to make things easier, or one on the other side of the world so you can combine it with a holiday?

Some points to bear in mind when choosing:

- **Time of year:** Think about how you'll cope with hot or cold weather. If you're a beginner runner from the UK, you are likely to struggle with a marathon in a hot country.

- **Travel and jet lag:** If you do decide to run a marathon abroad, remember that you may suffer from jet lag on arrival, so it's sensible to travel a few days in advance to give yourself a chance to adjust to the time zones.

- **Difficulty of the course:** Some marathons, such as Athens and Boston, are more difficult than others because of the terrain. Remember to bear this in mind when choosing which one to apply for.

- **Facilities and support:** How much support do the organisers offer?

- **Number of runners:** A smaller field of runners may feel less intimidating for the beginner. But remember this can also mean less support along the way.

- **Where to stay:** Do think about this well in advance as hotel rooms will quickly become booked up for the big marathons.

- **Practicalities:** Some of the marathons abroad have stricter qualifying standards, or require a doctor's certificate, for example, so make sure you're aware of these restrictions.

Top tip £££££££££££££££££££££££££££££££££

If you do decide to take part in a marathon abroad, Sports Tours International can help organise your trip. Visit **www.sportstoursinternational.co.uk** for more information, or phone 0161 703 8161. They also organise trips to other sporting events all over the world.

International marathons

Place	Month	Approx size	Website
Rome	March	6,000	**www.maratonadiroma.it**
Boston	April	10,000+	**www.bostonmarathon.com**
London	April	30,000+	**www.london-marathon.co.uk**
Paris	April	20,000+	**www.parismarathon.com**

Prague	May	3,000	www.pim.cz
Stockholm	June	12,000+	www.stockholmmarathon.se
Berlin	September	20,000	www.berlin-marathon.com
Amsterdam	October	2,000	www.amsterdammarathon.nl
Chicago	October	30,000+	www.chicagomarathon.com
Dublin	October	10,000	www.dublincitymarathon.ie
New York	November	30,000	www.nycmarathon.org
Honolulu	December	30,000	www.honolulumarathon.org

The box above shows just a few of the hundreds of marathons that take place every year around the world and might provide you with a starting point for thinking about where you'd like to go and run. If you have a particular destination in mind, you can almost guarantee they'll have a marathon, so look online on sites like:

www.aims-association.org,
www.runnersworld.co.uk,
www.marathonguide.com and
www.findamarathon.com for more.

For a really unusual marathon experience, how about one of these?

- **The Rock and Roll Marathon, San Diego.** With rock bands and cheerleaders performing every mile or so, and a huge concert afterwards, this has to be one of the most fun marathons around. **www.rnrmarathon.com**

- **The Walt Disney World Marathon.** Run through the Walt Disney World® theme parks, the Magic Kingdom® and Animal Kingdom® alongside your favourite Disney characters. www.disneyworldsports.disney.go.com

- **The Ice Marathon.** Not for the faint-hearted, this Antarctic marathon takes place in December at 80 degrees South. The only marathon of its kind, it provides a serious challenge for adventure marathoners. www.icemarathon.com

- **The Safaricom Marathon** takes place at the other end of the climatic scale, inside Kenya's Lewa Wildlife Conservancy, which is 5,500 feet above sea level and home to elephants, rhino, buffalo, zebra and many others sorts of game. www.lewa.org/lewa_marathon.php

- **Marathon du Medoc.** The gastros' marathon, this is run château-to-château through the vineyards of one of the most famous wine regions of France, being fed oysters and beef along the way. All finishers are presented with a boxed bottle of wine and the first and last runners receive their own body weight in wine. www.marathondemedoc.com

Top tip £££££££££££££££££££££££££££££££

You can find masses of information on all these marathons as well as many more, including half-marathons and shorter runs, at **www.runnersworld.co.uk**. They also have training advice and schedules, an active forum, first-hand accounts and the low-down on everything from what to eat to how to choose your footwear.

UK marathons

There are lots of marathons around the UK. Whether you're based in the Isles of Scilly or Loch Ness, Shakespeare country, Robin Hood country or on the Isle of Wight, you should have no problem finding a local race to take part in. It might be a good idea to do one of these for practice before taking part in a bigger and more daunting marathon.

If you do decide to do this, make sure you leave enough recovery time between marathons – six weeks at least, and longer if you're not an experienced runner.

Find a marathon local to you on **www.runnersworld.co.uk** or by contacting your local running club.

Getting a place in the London marathon

Because the London marathon is so over-subscribed, you can't just reserve a place. There are two main ways of getting one of the coveted spots.

- Some places are allocated using a ballot system. You pick up a copy of the entry form from JJB Sports, First Sport or a specialist running shop, and submit your entry for the ballot in the autumn – the deadline is usually in October. Check the website for details on **www.london-marathon.co.uk**. If you are lucky enough to get a place through the ballot, you'll usually hear in late November, and then that's it: you can just choose a charity to support, or a number of charities, and start raising your sponsorship money.

- If you don't manage to secure a place through the ballot

you will need to see if you can get one of the charity places. These are places that are bought by the charities who then allocate them to runners who commit to raising a set amount of money for that charity. Contact your favourite charity and see if they have places available.

If you can't find a charity with places, try the Charity Runners Clearing House [01923 440071 **www.charity-marathon.org.uk**] which matches runners to charities and keeps a list of charities with available places and the amount of sponsorship you'll need to pledge to raise.

It may also be possible, if you're a member of a running club, to get a place this way as UK Athletics-affiliated clubs are entitled to a limited number of places. However, most clubs will stipulate that you must have been a paid-up member for a certain amount of time in order to secure one of their places, so it is not a last-minute option.

Top tip ££££££££££££££££££££££££££££££££

Be aware that you have a commitment to the charity you are running for – your golden bond place in the marathon is reliant on the money you raise. If you don't make it you will have to pay them out of your own pocket.

Look at the official Flora London Marathon website [**www. london-marathon.co.uk**] for training advice, a dedicated forum for first-time marathon runners, and lots of other support and information.

Training

Training for a marathon is a big commitment. It takes lots of time, dedication, hard work, and running in the cold while everyone else is in bed or in the pub.

But if you're prepared to put the hours in, those who have done it swear nothing compares to the thrill of crossing that finishing line.

Top tip ££££££££££££££££££££££££££££££

London marathon runner Julia Williams, aka 'Marathon Mum', was a novice runner and mother of four when she agreed to take part in the 2005 London marathon to raise money for Tadworth Court Children's Trust. She successfully completed the marathon and wrote a blog [**www.marathonmum.com**] and a book about her experiences.

Julia says: "Get some serious running under your belt before you aim for the marathon – in hindsight I should have built up slowly. So starting at least a year before is a really good idea."

Julia's advice for newbie runners is:

- Start slow and see where you go. If you can't run all the way, run/walk. There are loads and loads of good programmes if you go online. I'd recommend **www.realbuzz.com** and **www.HalHigdon.com**.

- Drink! Always make sure you're fully hydrated, particularly in summer. I have found, through trial and error, it's best (particularly if running in the early morning) to drink plenty the night before and drink an hour before you run, to allow for loo breaks. Otherwise dire things happen, particularly when you've had children . . .

- Ice against injury. One tip I was given by a professional footballer is to sit in a bath of cold water after a run. It does take some doing, but it damps down inflamed muscles and helps avoid injury.

- If you do get injured, rest it, elevate it and ice it. If it doesn't get better, seek medical advice. If it doesn't improve, don't push it. If you have to pull out, you have to pull out (ditto if you're ill).

Top personal trainer Michael Garry has years of experience helping people reach peak fitness and has worked in some of London's best hotels as resident exercise guru.

Here is his Beginner's Guide to marathon training.

Running the marathon (26.2 miles) is the ultimate goal for many runners. To help make sure you complete the race and have an enjoyable experience depends mainly on how you prepare. I would suggest that before considering entering a marathon that you run on a regular basis covering distances ranging from 5k to a half marathon for at least six months to a year. This should allow time for the body to adapt and get stronger for all the training ahead. Here are a few tips to help you towards a successful race.

Getting started

- Follow a schedule. Try using the novice training plan in *Runner's World*.

- Always warm up and stretch, ideally for 10 to 15 minutes, before running and cool down and stretch afterwards.

- Follow the hard/easy rule: if you train hard one day, take it easy the next. If you develop an injury, rest for two days, then try to run. If you're still having problems, rest for a further day or two and if the pain persists, seek professional advice. If you get an injury, take time off. A sports massage will help you to recover and relax tight muscles.

- On long runs, check that you are not training too hard. Use a heart-rate monitor to help to ensure that you stay at between 60 and 70 per cent of your maximum capacity. To work out your heart rate, subtract your age from 220. (If, say, you are aged 40, this will give you a figure of 180.) Multiply this by 60 per cent. (At 40, this would mean 108 beats per minute. At 70 per cent of capacity it would be 126 a minute.)

- Never increase mileage by more than 10% per week.

- Start strength training, focus on core legs, and upper body strength twice a week.

- A diet rich in complex carbohydrates is important. Go for wholemeal breads, wholemeal pasta, pulses, grains, fruit and vegetables. Oats are particularly good for breakfast. But if you are running first thing in the morning, have only a light snack.

- Train yourself to drink and run at the same time, to keep your body hydrated. Garry suggests getting your body used to drinking a sports drink because these are handed out on the day and can make some people feel sick if they are unused to them.

- Train with friends. Long runs can take it out of you, so it is good to have company. For women especially, running alone in the dark is not safe.

- Wear the right running shoes. Try a specialist store such as Run and Become (in London, Edinburgh and Cardiff).

- Don't wear new trainers on the big day. Make sure that all your kit is tried and tested otherwise something may rub and cause discomfort. Six weeks' use before the run is about right for shoes.

- Try to run a half-marathon first to give you an idea how the full one will feel.

Top tips £££££££££££££££££££££££££££££££££
from the London Fitness Consultancy

Keep it varied

'Fartlek' is Finnish for 'speed play' – it means going out for a run and making it up as you go, mixing fast with slow, walk with run, hills with flat. Enjoy them.

Intervals help to improve your fitness and increase your pace. Run them at a pace that means you can complete the session. For one-minute efforts recover for one minute with a walk. Equate the recovery time to the effort time on the other sessions.

Vary the surfaces on which you run. Grass is kinder on joints but remember that in the race you run on road.

Don't forget to stretch

Stretching before and after each run is important – especially hamstrings and calf muscles.

Fancy dress. Every year there are hundreds of marathon runners taking part in the London marathon in ever-wackier costumes. Some people have found that sponsors are more generous if you're prepared to get dressed up in a silly outfit.

Good for extroverts, it can make sure you and your charity stand out from the crowd – you may even get on TV – but remember that a heavy or restrictive costume can be really hard to run, or even walk, in.

Do try it on well in advance and make any necessary adaptations to make it easier to move around in.

Top tip £££££££££££££££££££££££££££££££

If you're running in a heavy costume, train with a weighted rucksack to help you get used to carrying the extra load.

If you're keen to go down the fancy dress route, here are some ideas to get you going. Think links: how can you link your costume to your charity? It can provide the media with a neat 'hook' for a story, and you can use it effectively in your own publicity. For example, fundraisers for the Anthony Nolan Trust have run in daisy costumes – the symbol of the bone marrow trust.

Make sure you display your charity name clearly on your costume.

A few costume ideas:

- Angels
- Animals
- Batman and Robin
- Braveheart
- Bunny girls
- Cartoon characters
- Cowboy
- Doctors
- Elvis
- Leek
- Marilyn Monroe
- Nurses
- Pirate
- Prisoner
- Runaway bride
- Superman
- Wombles
- Wonderwoman

Ready, get set . . .

- Taper your training in the run-up to the race – you don't want to go into it tired from over-training. A short, gentle run the day before will help get rid of any tension.

- Get your running clothes ready in advance so you can be confident you have everything you will need on the day.

Top tip ££££££££££££££££££££££££££££££

Eat more carbohydrates during the week before the race to increase glycogen stores. Otherwise, keep your diet the same as during training, as making last minute changes could cause you problems during the race. *Michael Garry*

- Eat a well-balanced dinner the night before and relax with a good book or film..

- Make sure you know how the event is going to be organised, start points, where you have to be when, and what to do at the end of the race. Major marathons should make all of this information easily available, and it's often on their websites.

Make sure you know how the event is going to be organised, start points, where you have to be when, and what to do at the end of the race. Major marathons should make all of this information easily available, and it's often on their websites.

Go! On the day

So, Marathon Day has finally arrived, you've got your sponsorship pledges, you're fit and uninjured (hopefully) and raring to go. Think positive – you've been preparing for this for a long time, you *will* finish.

- Grease up with Vaseline anywhere you might chafe or blister, and cover your nipples with surgical tape.

- Make sure you're up and ready in good time, and plan how you're going to get to the start line in advance – you don't want to be rushing and arrive flustered or late.

- Don't use any drinks or supplements like glucose tablets that you haven't used during training.

Ten things about the marathon that you don't see on TV, from Julia Williams, the Marathon Mum:

- It is really, really weird running through red traffic lights.

- The sound of the slap of people's feet enters your psyche somewhere deep, so it ends up being the sound you hear when you go to sleep on marathon night.

- There are showers on route, which you run through when you are hot – it is a bit like going through the human equivalent of a car wash.

- It is possible to run in time to whatever piece of music you hear en route – any music at all immediately cheers you up.

- The miles seem to pass quicker than you thought, except when you miss the mile markers.

- It is possible to still smile and laugh when all your muscles are screaming.

- I said to someone at the start I've done a labour of 26 hours so 26 miles can't be as bad – and I was right.

- I felt like I did after I gave birth, but with the advantage that I don't have to get up in the night.

- I have never been in a crowd that exuded such good nature and support.

- Nothing can compare to the magical feeling of finishing.

Justgiving

Since its launch in the UK in 2001 over £127,000,000 has been donated through the Justgiving website and Firstgiving (the company's American arm) and it's become the standard way for people undertaking sponsored fundraising to collect money. Fundraisers set up their own pages, a process which is made simple by step-by-step instructions, and it's easy to personalise them, add photographs and keep track of your totals. In addition, donations made by UK taxpayers via the site are eligible for Gift Aid, which means that the charities can reclaim the 28% tax.

You can only use Justgiving to fundraise for one of the 16,000 + charities registered with them, not for other projects for which you might be trying to raise money. If you're raising money for a registered charity that isn't signed up to Justgiving yet, it's easy for them to do so for an affordable monthly charge, and it means they can reclaim Gift Aid on every £1 donated through the site. Visit **www.justgiving.com** for more details.

Where do I start?

Set up and personalise your page online by following the instructions given at **www.justgiving.com**. You can then give the website URL (address) to friends and family and anyone other potential sponsors.

Don't forget to put the URL on any website or blog you have set up, and also as an email signature if applicable.

Top tip £££££££££££££££££££££££££££££££££

I just hate asking for sponsorship money. Justgiving makes it much easier. *'Marathon Mum' Julia Williams*

Justgiving's tips

The team at Justgiving Towers have gathered a wealth of information about the most effective ways to use their site. You can read more about what other fundraisers are doing and gets lots of helpful hints on their blog at **www.justgiving .typepad.com**. In the meantime, here's some advice from Justgiving.

Pick a memorable URL

Do give plenty of thought to your Justgiving URL. Availability means you won't always be able to just have your name. So think of some memorable examples that will help your sponsors remember where your page is. Make them as intriguing as possible and you're going to multiply your click-through rate, which ultimately helps your fundraising total.

So keep it short and memorable. Avoid really long URLs in case people type it in wrongly and avoid underscores and hyphens because they can cause confusion too.

Personalise your page

Pages that aren't personalised raise much less money than their nicely decorated peers. There really is no excuse for not putting your own photo on these days. And make it a good one. An action shot maybe, something relevant to your event, your charity, or something that your sponsors will recognise.

A good photo helps communicate what you're doing and who you are (try and use one that is clear enough so that people will recognise you, rather than having to struggle to identify a tiny blurry face). And smile!

If you're PC-handy you could even add text captions to a photograph, or use a cartoon instead. There are loads of options, so use your imagination to come up with a really eye-catching image.

Justgiving provides you with a standard message for your page, but don't just use that – personalise it. You can keep their template but add in information about you, what you're doing and why. This is your chance to enthuse people and encourage them to give that little bit extra, so make use of it.

The Justgiving team have all sorts of ideas and guidance on how to do really whizzy things like include animated images on your page on their regularly updated blog, so do check this out as well.

Communicate your cause

It sounds really obvious but *so many* people forget to do it. Get the facts from your charity and find out exactly what a donation can pay for.

When you've got halfway to your target, update your blog and email your supporters, tell them what that money has achieved and what a difference the full amount will make. It is already in a charity bank account, after all.

Stagger your emails

Let's say you've got 100 contacts you plan to email your fundraising page to. Within that potential donor pool, you'll have maybe five or more different types of person: close family, extended family, some colleagues, a few old school friends and your best mates, for example.

You can't treat all of these people the same in your emails. Close family and friends, such as your mum, dad, husband, wife and pet rabbit, should always be the first port of call. They need to get the page started with a bang.

Once they've done their bit and put some decent money onto the page then you're free to craft your communications to the 'maybe' crowd. Due to the law of averages, your sponsors will look at the amounts others have donated and probably go for a similar figure.

Without that more personalised approach at the start, you could be stuck with a page that has a lower average donation.

Business cards

A business card with your Justgiving URL is great for lots of reasons:

- They fit in your wallet

- They're not sponsorship forms, so no hassle

- You can make them look nice

- You'll get sponsorship from people in the pub whose email address you don't have

- They're still not sponsorship forms

Top tips £££££££££££££££££££££££££££££££

for marathon fundraising

Ask well in advance. I was so worried I wasn't going to finish the marathon I didn't ask for money soon enough, as I didn't want people to think I was taking the mickey.

Definitely use the internet – I didn't have my blog then but I was on a couple of e-groups and many of my friends there were very generous.

I think the key is to not fleece everyone you know, which is what I hate about sponsorship. *'Marathon Mum' Julia Williams*

Other sponsored events

If you're not the marathon-running type – and let's face it, many of us aren't – there are still hundreds of things you can do to raise money through sponsorship. Don't forget, you can set up a Justgiving page for any kind of sponsored challenge as long as it's in aid of one of their registered charities.

Top tip ££££££££££££££££££££££££££££££££

Experienced fundraiser Susan Hill says: "The wackier the event the better. Or the braver. I always sponsor people jumping out of planes in parachutes, especially if they have never done it and people diving deeply and people trekking across the polar icecap. On the other hand there are a lot of sponsored walks and similar, with all the major charities running these already. So try and think of something new to catch people's attention and really maximise your sponsorship potential."

If you're interested in doing a parachute jump for charity, contact the British Parachute Association to find your local centre, at **www.bpa.org.uk** or on 0116 278 5271.

Sponsorship ideas

Countryside

- Clay pigeon shooting
- Fishing
- Poultry plucking
- Sheep shearing

BRIGHT IDEA

Turn your hobby or boring chores into ways to raise money.

I took my batty ex-racehorse round 20 miles of gallops at

Newmarket and raised £2,000. The previous year I did a sponsored muck-out and tack clean and raised £500 for Riding for the Disabled. *Suzy Baker*

Good for children

- Assault course
- Blindfolded for a day
- Bounce – on a trampoline or bouncy castle
- Hop
- Leap frog
- Poetry learning
- Pram push
- Read

BRIGHT IDEA ☀

Good challenge for kids during the summer holidays – read a set of books by one author, or a particularly long book.

- Recorder playing marathon
- Silence – even better for the parents ...
- Spell-a-thon with prize for the top speller
- Swim
- Swing push

BRIGHT IDEA ☀

The swing push could be a fun event for those trying to raise money to revamp a play area. You could also have a sponsored seesaw, roundabout, or even skateboard if you're trying to build a skate park.

- Toddle
- Tricycle ride
- Yo-yo

Musical

- Organ marathon

BRIGHT IDEA 💡

Playing the organ is a great way to raise money for church restorations.

- Piano marathon
- Rap marathon, get sponsored for every minute you can rap
- Singing or yodelling for a day

Pub style

- Darts marathon
- Pool/snooker
- Yard of ale drinking

CASE STUDY

Turn a single event into a larger one – let it expand, like Mair James did. A weekend of events, such as a shark dive, raffle and hog roast, raised nearly £3,000. This was added to an earlier sponsored abseil which raised over £500, and a sponsored zip wire which pulled in over £400.

"We did a weekend of fundraising which involved a sponsored carpet push," says Mair. "We donated the roll of carpet, and notified the local businesses in person what we were going to

be doing. Then we got six volunteers (all of whom who had got their own sponsorship) to push the roll of carpet the four miles around the village on a trolley. One person had a bucket and stopped all the cars on the way.

We counted up the money in a pub. People saw us doing this and added to the pot. Then we held an evening of entertainment, with a raffle of prizes including a pleasure flight and rugby memorabilia. The pub donated a hog roast which enabled the profits from this to go to the charity. And then we auctioned the roll of carpet!

The local press got involved, and the charity supplied T-shirts for everyone taking part."

Mair James

Sports

Instead of just a run or a walk, try and think of an interesting way of 'framing' the challenge. For example, cycling from London to Brighton, running the length of the London Underground's Northern Line, or running from one end of your county to another.

Also think of other ways you can keep it interesting – maybe doing it wearing something unusual, or carrying something (or someone). This is what catches people's interest – something they haven't seen or heard of before.

There are lots of annual sporting and outdoor events that you can take part in to raise money. Here are some of the major ones used by UK charities for fundraising:

Running in the UK

- London Marathon
- Great North Run
- Edinburgh Marathon
- Great South Run
- Great Manchester Run
- Reading Half Marathon
- Robin Hood Marathon & Half Marathon (Nottingham)
- Hydro Active Women's Challenge (various locations)
- Dublin City Marathon
- Belfast City Marathon
- The British 10K London
- Loch Ness Marathon
- Bristol Half Marathon
- Bath Half Marathon
- Liverpool Half Marathon
- Resolution Asset Management Women's 10K (Glasgow)
- City of Aberdeen Baker Hughes 10K
- The Great Scottish Run
- Great Edinburgh Run

BRIGHT IDEA ⫶🔆

When I was raising money for Race for Life I found people like to make it a challenge. For example my husband sponsored me in a complicated manner – he gave me £1 for every minute I was under an hour and then doubled it. *Elizabeth Thompson*

Running events – international

- New York City Marathon
- Paris Marathon
- Boston Marathon
- Berlin Marathon
- Chicago Marathon
- Marathon Des Sables
- Beijing International Marathon
- Prague Marathon
- Stockholm Marathon

Walking events – UK

- Coast to Coast
- West Highland Way
- Hadrian's Wall
- Four Peaks Challenge
- Three Peaks Challenges
- Yorkshire Three Peaks
- Great Wee Scottish Walks

Other events

- The London Triathlon
- Coast to Coast Bike Ride
- London to Paris Bike Ride
- Land's End to John o'Groats Bike Ride

In addition, individuals and teams choose to participate in local events or challenges to fundraise for their desired charity. Running events, triathlons and adventure races are commonly used to raise funds. There are thousands of UK and overseas events each year to choose from, which can be found in the time outdoors events calendar: **www.timeoutdoors .com/events/**

Other sporting or racing ideas

- Aerobathon

- Car, lorry, fire engine or van pull. Firemen and bin-men sometimes do these successfully. Needs hefty muscles, and you must clear it with the relevant authorities.

- Circle Line race

- Juggling

- Keepy-uppy

- Monopoly board – visit as many destinations as possible in a set amount of time.

- Slow bicycle race – how slowly can you compete a course without falling off?

- Wheelie race – bicycles, tricycles, dolls' pushchairs, wheel-chairs, skateboards, unicycles – anything on one or more wheels

- Winter swim in the sea

Good for offices

- Dress down day

- Fancy dress day

- Hair removal – head shave/beard shave/grow a beard or moustache/back wax

- Silly tie day – get sponsored to wear the most tasteless tie you can find

- Swear box

Dressing up

- Back to front clothes

- Ballerina day – Wear a tutu over your clothes

- Bling day – collect the sparkliest jewellery you can find and bling up your uniform or clothes

- Boys in bikinis

BRIGHT IDEA 💡

Encourage the boys in bikinis to undertake a sponsored swim.

- Clothes swap

- Drag day

- Handcuffed – spend a day handcuffed to a classmate or colleague, but don't lose the key!

- Hats and headgear

- Pyjama party

- Underwear Over Your Clothes Day

CASE STUDY

Becky Magson dressed up as a rabbit for the day to raise funds for the Hillside Animal Sanctuary and raised over £100.

She says: "I threw around many ideas typical of sponsorship events but I knew that incorporating something related to the reason for the fundraiser was paramount. The majority of animals at the sanctuary are farm animals, although they do have rescued pets, including rabbits. That was when I decided that dressing up was a real attention-grabber. Being a small animal owner myself, and also as the owner of a pet advice website [www.cavycapers.com], I decided to ask people to sponsor me to be a Bunny for a Day.

I wrote up my own press release, including a photograph of myself dressed up as a bunny, and sent it off to the local newspapers and national animal related magazines I knew of. I highlighted the connections and reasons for the event, the fact that I was an animal lover and owner, and the owner of a pet advice website wanting to help animals in need. The press release was well received, with some of the magazines agreeing to run the story and a reporter who worked for several local newspapers sending out a photographer.

I wrote to companies who I already deal with through my website, or related businesses, asking for a pledge of money or stock. In return for donations I offered publicity for their company through that generated by the bunny event.

I also printed up some posters advertising my Bunny for a Day event including a small section explaining why I was doing it. I wanted to pull on people's heart-strings by describing the sorrowful plight of many rescue animals.

I allowed around three weeks for preparation of the day, but with hindsight it may have benefited from a few more weeks to raise awareness and cash. I would definitely have worked on more local businesses for their support by asking for company donations or even to see if they would allow a collection box for the cause to sit in their business reception. I feel these are avenues I could have better exploited.

I've left the option open to do it all again. I found the whole experience exciting, challenging, fun and very rewarding. The success of my Bunny for a Day proves that just one person can still make a difference."

Services

- Car wash. Get a group together and ask your local supermarket (as long as they don't already have a car wash facility) if you can wash cars for cash. Supermarkets are especially appropriate as you will probably be covered by their public liability insurance (check this with them). Attract attention to your venture by playing some music (*Car Wash*, anyone?) and wearing silly hats or T-shirts.

- Dog walk for friends.

- Ironing. Get sponsored for every item you iron in a set time. Make it interesting – make it 'extreme ironing' in an unusual location.

- Shoe shining.

- Shopping bag carry.

Food

- Baked bean or custard bath.

- Cocktail stick challenge. How many peas, baked beans or other small food can you eat with a cocktail stick in a set amount of time?

- Cream cracker eating competition.

- Doughnut eating competition (no lip-licking allowed).

- Fast. A great idea to raise money for charities working in countries where food is scarce. Don't let young children fast as it's not good for them.

- Marshmallow marathon

- Onion peeling challenge

- Spaghetti junction – how many metres of spaghetti can you suck up in a set amount of time? Get sponsorship per centimetre or other measurement. Don't forget to measure it out before you begin.

- Worst meal challenge – get sponsored to eat all your least favourite things in one meal.

Give it up

- Your bed for a night. Sleep outside to raise money for a

charity that helps the homeless, perhaps.

- Your car. Get to work a different way every day for a week – on foot, by bus, on a skateboard . . .

- Chocolate

- Computer games

- Junk food

- Using the lift at work

- Nail biting

- Smoking

- Television

- Texting

Challenges

- Double Your Money Challenge. Ask people to take a small amount of money – a few pounds – and double it in any way they can. Record all the different things people have done. You might be able to get an employer or local business to match the amounts.

- Pen Swap Challenge. Buy a box of Biros, mugs or t-shirts printed with the name of your charity or cause. People buy the items from you for whatever it takes to cover your costs, and the challenge is on. They have a set amount of time to swap the original items for something else, and then swap that thing for something better, and so on. When the time is up, gather everything together and auction the swapped items, with a prize for the person who has achieved the best swap result. One man recently turned a red paperclip into a house using this trading technique.

- Matchbox Challenge. Collect as many small items as possible that will all fit into a matchbox. Get sponsorship for each item and a prize for the person who fits the most things into their box.

Major missions

As well as the smaller community-based sponsored events that take relatively little organisation and are often suitable for children to do, some intrepid individuals also undertake sponsored journeys and expeditions on a much larger scale.

Three such adventurous souls have agreed to share the benefit and wisdom of their experiences here. They are:

Richard Birch, who has taken part in two major journeys so far, one with Team Mongolian Job, a group of six men who travelled from London to the Mongolian Rally in 15-year-old Fiat Pandas, taking in five mountain ranges, two deserts and almost 8,000 miles, and one with Team Curried Away, who challenged themselves to get from the southern tip of India to Darjeeling (almost 4,000km) in as short a time as possible travelling in rickshaws (or "hairdryers on three wheels"). The missions [**www.team-mongolian-job.com** and **www.curried-away.co.uk**] have raised thousands of pounds for Send a Cow, Mercy Corps and Save the Children.

Antonia Bolingbroke-Kent who, with her friend Jo Huxter, drove a tuk tuk from Bangkok to Brighton (becoming the official world record holders for the longest ever journey by auto-rickshaw) and raised well over £30,000 at the time of writing in aid of Mind, the mental health charity. They have written a book about their journey [**www.tuktotheroad.co.uk**] and spoken at the Royal Geographical Society.

Dave Cornthwaite, of BoardFree, undertook two long-distance skates on a longboard. The first was from Land's End to John o'Groats, which served as a warm-up for the biggie – a 4,000-mile ride across Australia, from Perth to Brisbane [**www.boardfree.co.uk**]. He and his team have raised tens of thousands of pounds for Link Community Development, The Lowe Syndrome Trust and Sailability Australia.

The logistical challenges of some of these trips are enormous, and there isn't the space to deal with planning something like this in detail here. Nor are they appropriate for many fundraisers – they require a massive time-commitment, often a considerable amount of your own cash, the ability to withstand the rigours of sleeping in ditches and not washing for days on end.

But if you already have a fantastic idea for an unusual trip that you are burning to undertake, the collected wisdom of these travellers might help you on your way.

Some of the advice in this section is specific to those embarking on long journey type challenges, but a lot of it is also applicable to people raising money by any of the means already discussed, and more.

Choose your charity and set your target

Antonia says this should be the first step in your planning: "You can then start to dream up ways in which you are going to raise this money. With Jo and me these choices were easy as our idea had always been to drive a tuk tuk back to the UK from Thailand, and both of us had strong personal reasons to support Mind. Our original target was £100,000 but we quickly decided to downgrade this to £50,000 – still an ambitious amount but it was more realistic."

For some, the charity or cause will have been the initial motivator behind the challenge anyway. For others, the challenge is something you've thought of doing before, possibly for a long time, and it's then a matter of choosing which charity or charities you want to support.

If this is the case, make sure you bear two things firmly in mind when you're making your decision.

- It needs to be something you really believe in. Antonia feels that you should always "choose a charity that means something to you. If people see you have a personal relationship with the cause they are far more likely to donate."

- Do your research – Richard points out that you need to learn about the charities and the specific work your money is going to support. "Your sponsors will appreciate the information you can provide them. It also demonstrates that your motivations are as much for the charity as for the challenge."

Be brave and think big

If you're going to do something on this scale, you have to really go for it – you can't be half-hearted about it or it will fall flat. As Richard points out: "Seize the opportunity. If you're thinking of doing something seriously challenging, remember it might be your one big chance in life to raise lots of money. If the challenge is inspiring, people will react with awe, respect and most importantly, generosity. Don't be shy

– the money isn't being raised for you, it's for the causes you are supporting so don't be afraid to ask for people's support."

Plan, plan, plan

Often with a big event like this, the fundraising push is twofold. You need to raise funds to enable you to undertake the challenge and you need to raise money for the charity. There are different ways you can go about this. You can fund the challenge yourself if you can afford it, you can try and get corporate sponsors to shoulder most of the cost, or you can run earlier, separate, fundraising events to pay for the expenses.

Antonia ran various other events to raise money and says: "Fundraising events could be anything from a curry night to an auction of promises to a fancy dress dog show. Because I had past experience in putting on club nights and had contacts with some DJs and bands, we opted to put on a party at a club in London with a well-known band, DJs and a fantastic raffle. The latter alone raised £500. Be creative in your approach to fundraising. Think of ways to make people part with their money and get something out of it at the same time."

She also encourages fundraisers to apply the 'be bold' philosophy when thinking of ideas for events. "Don't be afraid to stand out and make a fool of yourself! Make people laugh – humour is key in getting people to support you."

Don't take anything for granted. Dave Cornthwaite warns: "Sometimes fundraising events can be costly. It's important to plan well to avoid making a loss on events. Never take for granted that just because you're organising a charitable event, venues will be willing to help you for free."

CASE STUDY

Dave Cornthwaite held all sorts of subsidiary events to raise money in conjunction with BoardFree.

He says: "Countless gigs, parties, BBQs (especially in Australia) and fêtes have been organised to complement the two main journeys, partly through appeals sent around for members of the public to carry out their own events on behalf of BoardFree. These events were an important part of raising awareness of the skate journeys and the charities we were supporting as well as funds. If an event was possible, often it was organised. A lot depended upon the enthusiasm of people willing to help out in particular localities.

Often the simplest and cheapest events were the most successful and enjoyable. Jumping on the back of other events, such as sporting occasions and already organised gigs and parties meant that expenditure was little but exposure and funds raised were maximised.

In all honesty, I can't remember an event that hasn't been enjoyable. We had a lot of BBQs in Australia which raised less than $50 (£20), but after a while it became obvious that purely judging events on funds raised at the time gave an inaccurate account of the event's success."

Publicity – get the most from the media

Make sure you investigate all avenues that might get you the right sort of publicity, from local newspapers, magazines and radio stations to larger, national publications. Don't assume they won't be interested – everyone in the media is looking for a story, and you never know......

Remember, if you don't ask you won't get.

Let your passion and enthusiasm shine through. The more you care, the more other people will be likely to as well.

Top tip ££££££££££££££££££££££££££££££££

"As with sponsors, events and celebrities, I ensured that I spent time researching all media outlets that might offer some coverage. Luckily, my journey was original and a world record breaking one, which of course helped coverage. I'm incredibly passionate about BoardFree and my journeys as a whole and I think this came across in interviews, which improved media coverage." *Dave Cornthwaite*

You can find more information on writing a press release in the chapter on *Publicity and media*, including a step-by-step guide on how to do it.

If you're planning an unusual journey, don't forget that you already have an interesting story that is likely to grab people's attention. Play on this.

Make sure your press release points to what is unusual and eye-catching about your challenge. Do the legwork for the people you are sending it to – no one wants to read a long-winded essay. Bullet points can help you keep it snappy if your tendency is to waffle.

Don't make it difficult for people to read or find information. Make sure your contact details are clear and easy to find.

Top tips £££££££££££££££££££££££££££££££

Make it catchy, make it funny. Revel in the uniqueness of the challenge.

If you've got the guts then make phone calls as they tend to have more success. If you do as much groundwork as possible then your chances of success are greater. For instance, a journalist is more likely to publish an item that is pretty much written already, than one that is just a set of notes. So write a short article and add additional notes/images.

The same applies when approaching radio or TV. Decision makers are busy so if they're given details about your challenge and are presented with some punchy questions and answers about it they're much more likely to be receptive to giving you air time as the preparation is already done for them. *Richard Birch*

Be nice, be polite, be friendly

Journalists are human beings and like anyone else, they're more likely to give space to your story and cause if they like you. Antonia supports this: "Make friends with your local press and get them to publicise your cause or any events you are putting on. Publicity is one of the best ways of raising money. We sent press releases off left, right and centre, and the local press were very supportive."

Asking for money

It's so very British to find this hard. But if you're going to be reticent and retiring about it, you won't reach your target.

Treat it like a business

This means networking. Ask anyone and everyone and ask them to ask others as well. The wider you spread the net, the more money and awareness you will raise.

Top tips £££££££££££££££££££££££££££££

Richard: Be direct, creative and persistent. I used the normal channels of friends and family, but tried to spread the net as wide as possible. Ask friends to email *their* friends and so on.

Antonia: Write a really good, punchy letter describing what you are raising money for and why and send it to as many people as you can think of. Family, friends, local businesses . . . the more people you write to the more money you will raise. Jo and I must have written about 400 letters in total.

Dave: Fundraising was an everything and anything solution. We wanted to maximise awareness and funds raised, so spread the word to friends, family, their friends and families. It was made clear that we wanted as many events as possible. We called it the 'BoardFree Blanket'.

Use your workplace

If you work in a large company, you have a golden opportunity for asking for help. Approach your firm and talk to them about ways you can ask your colleagues to support you. Richard, for example, gave a short presentation at a monthly 'all-staff' meeting.

"It gave me an audience of around 200 people," he says. "I delivered a light-hearted but compelling presentation which in turn led to loads of sponsorship. People were glad to listen because my presentation was far more refreshing than any work-related ones!"

Keep in touch

Once people have given you money or support, they are usually keen to keep up to date with your progress. A website or blog is an easy way to do this and, if well-written and entertaining, can become an important fund-raising and publicity tool. All three of the travellers featured here used the internet to great advantage, writing regular diaries of their trips, posting photographs and using the sites to ask for donations of equipment and providing links which made it easy for people to donate money.

BRIGHT IDEA

Keep your sponsors informed of your progress/the outcome of the challenge. Whether it's an internet site, intranet at work, newsletter, flyers or a slideshow down the pub, keep them informed. That way they'll feel a part of what you're doing and will appreciate it. *Richard*

Top tip ££££££££££££££££££££££££££££££££££

You can set up a blog for little or no cash. Easy-to-use sites include **www.blogger.com**, **www.typepad.com** and **www.wordpress.org**.

Charitable trusts

Don't ignore these as a possible avenue of funding.

BRIGHT IDEA

Find out if there are any charitable trusts in your area and when they meet. There are hundreds of these in the UK and they normally meet twice a year to decide where to distribute their funds. *Antonia*

The Association of Charitable Foundations provides guidance on applying to a charitable trust or foundation and an A-Z list of trusts in the UK, **www.acf.org.uk**.

Top tip ££££££££££££££££££££££££££££££££££

Look for support from your local authorities. In many cases, there are funds set aside from public budgets for certain projects. We qualified under a heritage budget for support from our district council.

Approaches to well chosen trust funds can be very fruitful, but there are two distinct stages: the first is to choose the right trusts, and the second is to produce the right application. I won't rehash anything here, but I read two books *Fundraising – From Grant Giving Trusts and Foundations* and *Avoiding The*

Wastepaper Basket and found them very helpful. *Sam Spreadbury, treasurer, Bassingbourn church roof appeal*

Three tips for approaching business sponsors

Spread the net wide

Antonia and Jo approached companies "mainly through having contacts within companies. Also pestering people and identifying companies who we thought would want to be associated with our slightly outlandish concept."

Ask for specific products

> **Top tip** £££££££££££££££££££££££££££££££
>
> "When approaching companies for sponsorship I found they are much more likely to donate products than cash. Your success rate will be much better if you target what you ask for. Products can still generate cash by being raffled off, auctioned or sold online – or might just be useful to help you complete the trip. I found that being direct and asking for specific products as a donation worked really well. *Richard*

Dave also found this. "Shoes, boards, clothes and other items were donated, often in quantities which would enable us to sell some off to raise more funds."

Offer them something in return

As with anything in life, people are more receptive to being asked for donations if they are also going to get something out of it.

Yes, you're raising money for charity, but so are a lot of other people, and companies receive many requests for support. Don't just assume that they will choose your challenge as the one to back – it is up to you to make it an attractive proposition.

BRIGHT IDEA 💡

In return I offered space on my website to plug the sponsor and space on the vehicles for a company sticker. By doing that companies can justify their contribution out of a marketing budget rather than out of a sponsorship/charity budget (which they may not have). *Richard*

Celebrity involvement

With journeys such as those described above the potential for celebrity support is different from some others. You're often not going to be asking them to attend an event or even donate anything. However, a positive quote from celebrities, especially those who have links or personal sympathies with the charity you are supporting, can be used to garner both media attention and more support. Antonia and Jo used quotes from celebrities such as Stephen Fry, Trisha Goddard and Melvyn Bragg on their website.

Antonia advises: "Find out which celebrities are associated with your charity and write to them via their agent. See if they will endorse what you are doing in any way, even a quote can help. Press in particular will prick up their ears if you have celebrity endorsement."

Remember that by asking a celebrity to give you a quote you are effectively asking for them to give your cause and project their 'seal of approval', so make sure you give them all the information necessary for them to do this. Tell them who you are, what exactly you are doing, and what you are asking for.

Dave managed to get celebrity support from a range of individuals.

"Celebrities always help to raise the profile and reputation of events," he says. "Ellen MacArthur, Bear Grylls, Tony Hawk, Rod Stewart and Penny Lancaster, Jono Coleman, Jonathan Ross and more offered quotes. Australians such as musicians Xavier Rudd and Ash Grunwald, as well as Neighbours actor Alan Fletcher, were more hands-on with their support, wearing BoardFree T-shirts, getting me on stage with them in Melbourne, Sydney and the Gold Coast, and even offering donations from CD sales."

See the chapter on *Celebrities* for more information on this subject.

The highs and lows of journeys like the ones described here can be extreme.

Some thoughts from Richard, Antonia and Dave.

The highs ...

Richard: "What I underestimated the most about these challenges was the fun of the preparation. It's just as well as the preparation is likely to last far longer than the challenge itself. Enjoy it. Setting a seemingly impossible goal and then achieving it is an excellent feeling."

Antonia: "The highs are the adventure, excitement, sense of achievement, all the wonderful people you meet."

... and the lows

Richard: "The fear of failure can weigh quite heavy. With big sponsorship comes an additional pressure to succeed. The thing I feared most with both challenges was breaking down right at the start and having to pull out. If this had happened, I'd have felt like I'd let all the sponsors down. Good preparation helps reduce the chance of spectacular failure.

"On these types of challenges, the 'expect the unexpected' cliché couldn't be more apt. During the London to Mongolia drive, I spent 24 hours in police custody in Kazakhstan after we showed up at a rarely visited border, to the bewilderment of the local authorities. I could never have anticipated that I'd be locked away, alone, for a night and rigorously questioned the following day, whilst my team mates sat and worried at the border. The main thing is to treat it all as part of the fun.

"I'd recommend that people enjoy every aspect of their challenge. Treat the fundraising, media work and challenge all with equal relish. There are plenty of new experiences along the way and I feel as if I've learned and benefited as much from doing a live radio show as I have from learning to drive a tuk-tuk; as much from doing a presentation to colleagues

about charity projects in far flung places as I have from trying to explain my reason for being at a Russian checkpoint
in a beaten-up English-registered Fiat Panda."

Tenacity

Dave says: "Don't ever give up. Be passionate, always
remember who benefits from the work you're doing and
when things seem hard just keep pushing, keep your chin up
and just do your best. Hard work, perseverance and a little
bit of initiative go a long, long way."

Grand events

Organising balls, banquets and other big bashes

A big party is often top of the list of many fundraising committees' ideas. It could take the form of a black tie ball, a medieval banquet in a castle, or a gourmet lunch and auction in a smart hotel or restaurant. Although these events can be a lot of fun and very lucrative, they require an enormous amount of planning, organisation and salesmanship if they are to go off with a bang rather than a whimper.

With any big bash, you must make sure you keep all the 'balls' in the air.

Your primary aim is to:

• Raise money and awareness for your cause.

In order to do this you will need to:

• Get people to come.

And in order to do this, you will need to:

• Plan, organise and execute an enjoyable event, so people are encouraged to give more money on the night (through an auction or raffle, perhaps), and that they would attend again if you ran another.

Meanwhile, you need to make sure that you get as much provided for free so that your profits are as large as possible. It is no small task then, but worth it.

Josette Falzon says the sellout gala dinners she helps organise are some of the most enjoyable events she's been involved with. She and her fellow organisers have worked out how to ensure they make money.

She says: "We try and strike a good deal with a 5-star hotel on a good menu and then top up the price by aiming for at least £6 profit for every person. We then also do a raffle with good prices like weekend breaks and flights – all given to us free of charge, obviously – and therefore can easily raise another £1,000 from the raffle on the evening."

CASE STUDY

The Wedding Dress Ball

Emma Wykes, one of the three women organisers of the Wedding Dress Ball, shares the lessons they have learnt about running a large charity fundraiser and her thoughts and tips on how best to go about achieving the above three aims.

Emma, Debs and Nikki first came up with the unusual idea of holding a party at which 'has-been' brides could wear their wedding dresses as they all felt it was sad that their beautiful and expensive gowns would otherwise languish in a wardrobe or attic.

Initially they had planned a small party at one of their homes, but shortly afterwards a good friend of one of the group was diagnosed with neuroblastoma cancer and they saw an opportunity to raise money for research into the disease.

They've raised over £5,000 at each Wedding Dress Ball. Ballgoers enjoy a five-course meal, a charity speaker to tell people about the cause that they're raising money for, then the raffle draw, followed by entertainment provided by a band and a disco.

Planning, organising and executing

The venue. This is one of the first things you need to decide on. Once you have the venue and the date confirmed, you can start to publicise your event. You'll also be able to establish how much of the organisation the venue will take care of, and what you need to do. It'll also affect things like music and entertainment, as, depending on how much space there is, there may only be room for a disco rather than a big band, for example.

Emma explains: "We decided on the venue early on, which I think influenced how the event was structured. Nikki and Debs had both been to events at York Racecourse before, so knew that they could cater extremely well and on a large scale. Debs also attends lots of other balls, so wanted to follow a similar theme."

Think carefully about the venue before you commit to using it. Some points to bear in mind when you're researching venues:

- Is it easily accessible?
- Will guests be able to get home easily at the end of the night?
- Is there enough parking?

- Does it have disabled access?

- Do the numbers add up? Find out exactly what will be included and what you have to provide.

- Is the room where you will be the right size?

- If you want to have drinks before the meal, will these be in a separate room?

- Check that the toilets are clean and pleasant.

- Is there a cloakroom for guests' use?

- Can they provide good food at a reasonable cost?

- Is there space for a band or disco? Is there a dance floor, or space for one?

- Do they allow fireworks, if desired?

- How do they usually arrange their tables?

- Ask for sample menus and wine lists when you first look around.

- What time they are licensed to serve alcohol until?

- Is there a public address (PA system)?

- Are there any noise level restrictions?

- Do they have a good reputation for running similar events – see if you can speak to previous customers.

- Check their cancellation policy. If you don't sell as many tickets as you had hoped and you are forced to cancel, you don't want to be lumbered with a large fee.

Responsibilities. Get your core committee together early on in the process and make a master list of jobs that will need doing. Then divide them up, making a note of who is in charge of what, and make sure that everyone is clear on what their individual tasks are and when they need to do them by. One person should take control of this list and be in charge of making sure that things get done – ticking off jobs on a list or a wall planner as they are achieved, or whatever you find most efficient. The important thing is that someone knows what has been organised and what remains to be done.

"For the first event, we all fell into roles that we were comfortable with," says Emma, "although we did dish some tasks out formally. There were only three of us involved on both occasions. I took on things like the written communication, involving raffle, sponsorship letters, website, meeting minutes and Debs, who's comfortable with figures, took on the money management and general promotion/advertising. Nikki managed the relationship with the racecourse and went out collecting some of the raffle prizes."

See the chapter on *Planning* for more on setting up committees.

Communication. During the run-up to the event, meet regularly so that any problems can be resolved sooner rather than later, and everyone knows what stage the plans have reached. A regular weekly or fortnightly email update to everyone would be a good idea.

Menu planning. When you're selecting the menu remember that you're catering for a large group of people all of whom will have different tastes and preferences. Make sure you are prepared for a variety of dietary requirements and always have a vegetarian option.

Emma says: "We went for a well established banqueting venue which is more than capable of dealing with lots of different dietary requirements. We had a general menu on the website, plus the vegetarian option, and a gluten free menu was available on request. We had some unusual requests as well, but all were catered for with relative ease.

"At the first ball we had some last-minute attendees who received different food from that advertised on the website and so weren't as pleased as they could have been. Another time we would tell anyone booking tickets at such a late stage that there might be limited menu choice."

Insurance, licences, parking. Another benefit of holding your event at a hotel or other large public venue that is already set up for banqueting is that there will be fewer issues with licences and parking, for example, than you might have to consider if you chose to hold your event in a marquee or on private property. If you do decide to run your event outside a banqueting venue, make sure that you contact your local council well in advance. They will be able to advise you on any licensing and health and safety regulations that you need to comply with.

But even within the relatively controlled setting of a hotel or other banqueting venue, if you're putting on any unusual entertainments, consider whether you need to get insured against accidents or mishaps. Emma warns: "We had a horse-drawn carriage at one Wedding Dress Ball. One of the horses actually stood on and tore one of the ladies' dresses slightly, so insurance against such freak occurrences might have been a good idea."

> **Top tip** £££££££££££££££££££££££££££££££££
>
> Public Liability Insurance protects you against someone sustaining an injury at your event and suing you. Any subcontractors at your event should have their own Public Liability policy as well. If you're running your event to raise money for an existing charity, or in a venue that holds similar events regularly, then you might be covered by their policy, but it's essential that you check this. You can find an insurance broker at BIBA – the British Insurance Brokers' Association.

Awareness. "When publicising the 2004 event," says Emma, "we spent a great deal of money on advertising, some of which was enormously helpful in increasing ticket sales, but some of which was a complete waste of money. I would advise people to try and get their local paper interested in printing a story about the event, rather than paying for costly advertising. Local papers, radio, and, if you're lucky, television, will be interested in an event that's different and exciting, so don't hesitate to get in touch with them. Once the original articles were out, we also attracted interest from a regional and finally a national publication – News of the World's Sunday magazine came along and took exclusive pictures and wrote an article."

Top tip ££££££££££££££££££££££££££££££££

Think about the timing of your publicity. Try and stagger it, so you have some in advance and some closer to the event. Don't rely on any publicity close to the date for selling tickets.

Emma says: "I did radio interviews and we appeared on our local regional BBC news programme. If we'd been able to get that publicity a few weeks before it would have been great, but as they wanted it really near to the event so we missed out on additional people who wanted to attend but who had found out about it too late."

A website is an ideal way of publicising your event, as well as a place to put important information for those attending.

Some things to consider putting on your website:

- Ticket information – the price and how to buy.

- Maps and directions to the venue.

- Start and end times.

- Contact details for the organisers, venue and local taxi services.

- Details of the evening – highlight any unusual entertainment or special prizes, for example.

- Menu, along with how to inform the organisers of any special dietary requirements.

- Mentions of any sponsors.

- Information about the charity, and how to find out more and donate money.

Ticket sales

- Work out your numbers early on in the process – how many you're catering for, how much the tickets will be and how many you need to sell to cover your costs and start turning a profit.

- Make sure you have a failsafe way for people to pay, and that they pay before attending the event. Assign someone the job of keeping tabs on all of this, and making sure the money is paid into a dedicated bank account as soon as it is received.

Emma says: "Debs worked out our ongoing costs and kept quite a tight rein on what we were spending. She worked out early on what our break-even point was, so we knew what we were aiming for. We were overambitious in the number of tickets we thought we would sell in 2004, but by 2005 we were much more realistic. We promoted how to purchase tickets on our website, but took payments by good old cheque or cash. We dabbled, very briefly, with PayPal payments, but the fees were so steep we had to nip this in the bud as it ate into the profit margins too much."

- Don't make the tickets too expensive. People won't come if they are too expensive, especially as they know they're going to be asked to spend more money on the night. It's far better to sell all your tickets for a slightly lower price, and have a successful event, where people dig a bit deeper on the night, than to make your tickets so pricey that not enough people come and the event is either disappointing or, worse, has to be cancelled.

Extras

"The main idea of the night is, of course, to make as much money as possible, which the sale of the initial tickets obviously helps along. On the night, we had buttonholes on sale for the men (which had been very kindly donated by a local florist) plus the raffle tickets. In 2005 we also had a silent auction of football memorabilia, which worked surprisingly well."

The raffle is a big part of the Wedding Dress Ball, with a range of tempting prizes. Good prizes will encourage people to buy plenty of tickets. As well as approaching local businesses for prizes, some people came to them with donations. "Some raffle prizes were donated by companies who had heard about the event in the local press," says Emma. "In 2004 a lovely lady donated 12 beautiful bouquets, one for each month following the ball."

- Prizes such as this will raise money from raffle ticket sales and potentially get more people interested in attending your event. So the more unusual and interesting prizes you can get your hands on, the better. Try and get a local company to print the tickets for free.

- Remember to offer businesses something in return for any donations or sponsorship. Can you produce a leaflet or brochure and include their details? Thank them publicly and on your website? If you can reassure them that they're not being asked to give something for nothing your requests will get a far more positive response.

- You could also auction prizes, particularly if you have a number of higher-value items donated.

- Consider asking a representative from the charity or cause to come and give a short talk about why the money is needed and what or who it will benefit.

At the Wedding Dress Ball, says Emma, this move went down really well. "Mik Scarlet is an actor, singer and journalist who happened to have neuroblastoma cancer as a child and was given pioneering treatment that cured his cancer but left him in a wheelchair. Mik came along and gave a powerful and amusing speech as we were going round selling raffle tickets. It certainly helped people get their hands in their pockets!"

On the night

- Again, assign individuals specific responsibilities.

- If you're running an auction or raffle, make sure you have worked out the logistics of it in advance.

"The on-the-night organisation was the one thing that we really felt we tripped up on at the first event," says Emma.

"Debs was taking the hat round for people to pick tickets from, I was calling the numbers and Nikki was handing out the prizes. However, because we didn't keep hold of the tickets and tried to run the draw too fast, there was a mix-up with a prize and a person who thought they'd won a major prize ended up with a bottle of whisky. So the next year we got more efficient and had a sheet printed out with each prize. Once the number had been called we stapled the winning ticket to the prize sheet and asked the winner to go to the prize table for Nikki to present them with their prize, There were no mix-ups and we'll be adopting this practice again in the future."

- Make sure you've done a table plan in advance, and that it's clearly displayed so people can find their tables and seats easily. If you have a large number of people attending, you might want to display two, or think of another way of ensuring there isn't a bottleneck of people huddled around one board trying to work out where they are sitting.

- Think about how you'll welcome people. Consider making it one person's responsibility to 'meet and greet' guests.

- Someone will need to be in charge of making any announcements, and possibly act as MC for the raffle or auction. Make sure you have a microphone and stand set up if necessary, and that the person can be seen and heard from everywhere in the room.

- Make sure you arrive at the venue in plenty of time so that you can check the room and decorations, and iron out any last-minute problems.

After the event. Ensure all the key people are thanked, including sponsors, guests, the owners of the venue, volunteers – everyone who has contributed to the smooth running of the evening.

Be original. The Wedding Dress Ball is an original concept, which stemmed from the girls' desire to wear their wedding dresses again. The best thing you can do to ensure a successful event is to come up with a similarly fun and inventive idea of your own – a new take on a tried-and-tested formula, a twist to add to a traditional event, or a different way of doing things.

BRIGHT IDEA 🔅

When brainstorming for ideas, try breaking the evening down into its component parts and thinking about new things you could do with each.

Here are some elements that might help your brainstorming:

Theme. A themed event, such as Oriental, circus, black and white, heaven and hell, a masked ball, Moulin Rouge, could get your event greater press coverage and give you a way of tying the food and decorations in together.

Dress code. Can you come up with an exciting dress code, or one that is relevant to your charity or area perhaps?

Tickets. Is there something you can do to make these stand out? Have the tickets printed on paper fans or balloons, for example.

Venue. An unusual venue could set the tone for the whole evening. Look in the Yellow Pages [**www.yell.com**] and get in touch with your tourist board to find them. The Landmark Trust [**www.landmarktrust.org.uk**] has details of many historically and architecturally interesting buildings which can be rented, and this might be something to investigate.

Food. Backwards dinners? A menu on a chocolate theme, with some of it in every course? Food 'stations' that people can visit through the evening rather than a sit-down meal? With a bit of thought and imagination, your dinner can step out of the everyday and become a real talking point –before, during and after the event.

Decoration. As well as flowers and lighting, quirky table decorations can add a huge amount to a sit-down dinner. Think about asking a business to donate things you can put at people's places as 'favours', or to put in goody bags to give guests as they leave.

Entertainment. Music is a must, but there are lots of other options for entertainment. Fun casinos, magicians, jugglers, cartoonists, jesters and fortune-tellers can all be hired to entertain guests.

Auctions and sales

Turning temporary tradesman can turn in a tidy profit for your cause if you get it right. As with all events, it's a case of thorough research, good planning and careful on-the-day organisation to make sure your sale is more of sellout than a washout.

CASE STUDY

Author Susan Hill helped organise a charity auction as part of a lunch in aid of the Prince of Wales Hospice in Pontefract. The day's proceedings raised many thousands of pounds for the hospice.

She came up with an unusual idea to raise more money in the auction.

"It's always a struggle to think up new fund-raising ideas but I wasn't thinking of fund-raising at all when I watched a cricket match in the village near my home at the beginning of the season and admired the brand new all-white baseball caps one team was sporting. They looked smart but I sat in the spring sun and thought how a graffiti artist would love to draw pictures all over them – and an idea was born!

I am a patron of The Prince of Wales Hospice in Pontefract, West Yorkshire, and was organising a huge fund-raising lunch in London that autumn. The Prince of Wales was coming and we were having an auction, for which my friend Stephen Fry had agreed / had his arm twisted, to be the auctioneer. Now all I had to do was get the items. When I got home I looked through that useful magazine Exchange and Mart until I found wholesalers of promotional items – mugs, T-shirts, and pens. There were plenty but no one seemed to do baseball caps so I had to research further, on the internet, until I found a manufacturer.

I bought a dozen white ones, having obtained the best possible price by explaining what they were for. I then wrote a great many letters to all kinds of celebrities, asking if they would decorate and sign a baseball cap for the auction if we supplied it. As usual, the percentage of replies was small – but the brilliant thing was that almost everyone who answered said 'Yes'. I had introductions to a couple of people via friends and I also shamelessly held friends of my own to ransom. Well, they do it to me all the time.

I sent out the baseball caps and after a few weeks they began to arrive back, fully decorated. And what caps they were.

Elton John had personally sewn Versace buttons all over his, having cut them off Versace garments he no longer wore.

Dame Judi Dench used nail varnish to decorate hers and even drew a Prince of Wales feathers logo on the front in slightly blobby fluorescent pink.

The artist and painter of the Beatles' '60s LP, Sergeant Pepper`s Lonely Hearts Club Band, Sir Peter Blake, did a work of art in black pen and ink, tiny drawings and writing, all over the cap.

And J.K. Rowling painted a ping-pong ball gold, stuck two silver-painted cardboard arrows through it to represent the

Golden Snitch, and signed the peak of the cap, 'Very poorly designed and executed by J.K. Rowling'.

Those, and others which celebrities had signed on the peak, were brilliantly auctioned by Stephen, who used them to raise several thousand pounds at the lunch. We also had a lot of fun."

Other items that you could buy, ask people to decorate and then sell on:

- Postcards which you can then exhibit – and ask people to guess which celebrity decorated each

- Plain white T-shirts

- Badges – you can buy kits for these

- Greetings cards

- Masks

Car boot sales

If you're thinking of holding a car boot sale, your first step should be to contact your local council. You may need a licence to hold a sale and if you do it's important that you organise that *before* you set a date and start publicising the sale.

Also, some councils will let you hold the sale in their car parks if you're running it on behalf of a charity, so you could solve the issue of a site for the sale at the same time.

When it comes to pitches, you'll need to decide:

- How many you have space for – remembering to allow some space for vans as well as cars.

- How you are going to arrange them/lay them out

- How much you are going to charge for the spaces.

Advertise the sale well in advance so people have time to book pitches and get their sale items together. Include a contact phone number so that people can book pitches.

Car boot sale or market checklist:

- Do you need a market licence?

- Do you have a suitable location and permission to hold your sale there?

- How many pitches will you sell, and how will you do this? How much will you sell them for?

- Is the site big enough? How many people do you expect to attend? Can you ensure enough do attend?

- Do you need/have public liability insurance?

- Do you have a safety representative, people to sell tickets, and a steward to organise entry and exit of vehicles and set-up of stalls?

- Will there be refreshment vans/stalls?

- How will the organisers communicate with each other on the day?

- Are there toilets on site?

- Are the exits and entrances adequate in size and number?

- Do you need to alert the police (you will do in case of traffic issues)?

- What will happen in case of heavy rain?

Charity stall at a regular market

If you live in one of the many cities and towns around Britain that have a regular market, approach the organiser to see if you can have a charity stall. Most larger towns have a council officer with specific responsibility for markets, small towns would probably need to be approached via the town clerk. You could sell anything you like on it, and joining in with an existing market in this way means you don't have any of the organisational headaches of running and promoting an event yourself. Less time and less risk, but with potentially just as much profit.

Book sales

These are always popular and although you won't make a fortune you can still make a tidy profit if you plan, plan, plan.

Top tip ££££££££££££££££££££££££££££££££

Authors only get a limited number of copies of their books free so are unlikely to have piles of them to give away. They also cost quite a bit to post and as writers get a lot of requests for free signed books don't be surprised if you don't get many positive responses.

Instead, write to publishers asking for any overstocks or odd-ments they might give you, and offer to collect or pay carriage. They will rarely take you up on it, but it's a nice gesture. They have more copies available than authors and you're more likely to be successful in your request. *Susan Hill*

As well as asking for donations of books from publishers and local people, look on eBay's *'Wholesale and job lots'* section, and then under *'Books'*, where there are job lots of books available (for collection only, often, because of postage costs) for very little money. You can then divide them up and sell them on at a profit.

Some old and antiquarian books can raise a surprising amount on internet auction sites like eBay [**www.ebay.co.uk**] or specialist second-hand book sites such as Abe Books [**www.abebooks.com**], so consider putting these to one side and holding a separate internet auction for them once you've had them valued. It's always worth finding out more about any first editions of hardbacks to see if they're collectable. You wouldn't want to sell a valuable book for 50p.

Consider finding a trustworthy dealer or second-hand book-seller to come and look through the books once you have col-lected them and alert you to anything particularly valuable. You might be surprised by the potential value of some of the items people have lurking at the back of their shelves, so do get someone knowledgeable to check.

Plan the layout of the sale carefully – don't just muddle everything together on one table.

Having separate sections for books makes it easier for both

the sellers and the buyers. A sensible way to sort books might be to have different tables for:

- Paperback fiction
- Signed copies
- Cookery books
- Biographies and autobiographies
- General non-fiction
- Parenting and childcare (if you have enough)
- Children's

Pricing

Don't over-price ordinary paperbacks and well-thumbed copies, but do make sure anything brand new or a bit unusual is priced properly. Look in second-hand bookshops to get an idea of what is reasonable.

Publicising

As well as the usual methods, look on the Provincial Booksellers Fairs Association [**www.pbfa.org**] for booksellers in your region, and write to them to let them know about the sale.

BRIGHT IDEA

Sell cakes or biscuits at coffee time at work. Link your biscuits to your cause. Sell cat- or dog-shaped biscuits in aid of an animal shelter, or pink and blue iced cookies for a baby-related cause. You can buy hundreds of different shaped cookie cutters from cake decorating suppliers and **www.splatcooking.co.uk**

Auctions of promises

With an auction of promises you're asking people to donate their time, skills and expertise, rather than giving an item or monetary donation. This can mean that you end up with some really unusual and imaginative lots that are difficult to put a value on, so ensure that they don't go for too little by putting a reserve value on them, especially any that are going to require a lot of time on the part of the giver.

Let your imagination really run wild when thinking of people to ask for donations – the most unlikely people or businesses can sometimes come up with fantastic offers.

CASE STUDY

Susan Hill's armchair auctions

"I ran one of these in Chipping Campden to raise money for the local cricket club. This is an event that works best in a village or other close community. You approach people and businesses for offers of things – an evening's babysitting, a case of wine, a meal at a local restaurant, all sorts of different lots – then list them with a reserve price if there is one and details of exactly what people are bidding for.

Make sure you describe the lots as accurately and as enticingly as you can. Then instead of attending an auction evening, people bid at home, filling in their bids on the sheet of paper which you have delivered to them (enlist some help from volunteers with this) and have them return it to you or a central point by a set date, on which the armchair auction closes. You sit in your own armchair at home and go through

the list peacefully, then notify the highest bidders. We raised about £5,000 doing this."

Some prize promises to get you started:

- Babysitting.

- Slave for the day.

- Chauffeur for the day, a drive in a classic car or a ride on a motorbike, flight in a plane or helicopter or hot air balloon.

- A sailing lesson or boat trip.

- Yoga, dance, golf, fishing, horse riding, ice skating or skateboarding lessons, sessions with a personal trainer.

- A cookery lesson, your freezer filled up with home cooked meals, a gourmet meal cooked and served in your home, cakes delivered to your house every month for a year, canapés served at your drinks party.

- Your portrait painted, you, your family or your pet photographed, your cartoon or caricature drawn, a pottery lesson and personalised pottery.

- A room in your house redecorated, your garden tidied up and weeded and your clutter taken to the tip, your car washed and valeted, your windows washed, your house spring cleaned, your ironing done for a month.

- A bouquet of flowers every month for a year.

- Loan of a holiday home, stay at a hotel.

- Local or Sunday paper delivered for a year.

- A massage, manicure, shampoo and blow-dry, a facial, or reflexology treatment.

- Tour of a football ground, television station, theatre, fire station......

- Website design services.

- Signed books and photographs.

- A day with a celebrity on set of their television show or other place of work, tour of the House of Commons with your MP.

- Theatre tickets.

- A week of pet sitting.

Do it yourself

For some years it was cookbooks (see the later section on *Ideas to be wary of* for more on these) and more recently it's been slightly risqué calendars, inspired by the WI women who stripped for a fundraising calendar and who were represented in the subsequent film of their story, Calendar Girls. I wouldn't like to attempt to predict what the next craze will be in the arena of money-spinning products such as these, but the principles will stay the same – if you have an interesting idea, you can successfully sell it in aid of your charity if you get the sums right.

In deciding to produce an item such as this, the 'bottom line' is crucial. You'll be very unlikely to be able to manufacture your product for free just because it's for charity, so some initial investment is likely to be necessary. This means you must be absolutely sure that enough people are going to want to buy your item, and for the right money, so that you don't end up out of pocket.

To this end, you must:

Do your market research

Make sure there is a market for what you plan to make. Check someone hasn't done something too similar. If there is a precedent set, as in the example of calendars, make sure the market isn't saturated with them. By the time this book comes out there may well be a new, hot, charity idea. If too many people have done the same thing recently, think again. You don't want to be left with a house full of boxes of mugs or calendars or books that you can't shift.

Also, if your idea is a brand new one, and you can't find anyone who has done it before, make sure that there isn't a good reason for that. It could be that people before you have investigated the idea and found that it won't work, for any number of reasons. So look into it thoroughly, from every angle you can think of.

If, after you have done this, you are sure that the idea is a good one and that you will be able to sell it, you then need to:

Do your sums

Obviously, the more you are able to persuade businesses or individuals to give their time and expertise in producing your item, the better. But there may well be some upfront costs.

Make sure that you get a number of estimates for any printing or production costs – they can vary wildly.

Don't get seduced into producing huge numbers of the thing that you may not be able to get rid of under the guise of its being much cheaper per item. Decide how many you think you can reasonably sell and then obtain the best possible price for that number.

Remember, it's no good producing 10,000 of your product for peanuts if you can only sell 1,000 of them. And don't forget to take into account postage and packing costs if you're planning on selling via mail order.

Making a quilt

Communities with a group of keen seamstresses have had success making quilts. People contribute a few squares each, and the end result is auctioned to raise money.

CASE STUDY

The Oakley Girls calendar

This was produced by a group of women from the Oakley Hunt, aged between 19 and 60, who got together to create a calendar of 12 high-quality images of them semi-naked, shot by top photographer John Angerson. As well as selling the calendars to raise money for the Thames Valley and Chiltern Air Ambulance and the Oakley Hounds, the original images were auctioned, to increase profits. So far they've raised more than £12,000.

Jenny Rivers, one of the Oakley Girls, says that the two most important things when undertaking a project like this are planning and keeping an eye on budget. They managed to get the costs of producing the calendar covered by sponsorship. "All the girls helped to find sponsors via friends, business contacts, and anyone else who might be willing to help us (with a little persuasion)."

She advises other hopeful fundraisers to be very professional in their approach and says that a website is invaluable for imparting a slick and efficient impression. "We designed our own letter heading and notepaper and created a website. Everyone we made contact with was more than happy to help us and we had each month of the calendar, as well as our website, sponsored and this covered our artwork and printing costs. So when we came to sell the calendars, all the sales were profit."

When it came to publicity, they discovered the value of spreading the net as wide as possible.

> *"Our photographer was really helpful with his contacts in the media, and once we got into the main press things seemed to escalate. We even had a Russian television station come and make a documentary about us. We also did a lot of cold calling, and with persistence appeared on local radio stations and in magazines and newspapers."*

Her final tip is to make sure you are aware of and ready for the sheer amount of work involved in a project of this nature.

> *"Get as many people as possible who are prepared to work hard in order to make things happen. It's a lot of hard work*

*to make money, and it doesn't happen overnight. My draw-
ing room was full of boxes of calendars and envelopes in
the run-up to Christmas – it was manic. But the joy of seeing all of those cheques fall onto the mat afterwards made
it all worthwhile, and so enjoyable."*

Bulb sale

Bulbs are something that can be extremely expensive to buy
in small quantities and far cheaper if you buy in bulk. You
can take advantage of this and buy them wholesale, divide
them up and resell them at a dedicated sale, or as part of a
fête or larger event.

Remember, bulbs need to be planted at certain times of the
year: spring-flowering bulbs in the autumn (September to
November) and things like dahlias and perennials in the
early part of the year (January to March). Two of the major
bulb suppliers are Peter Nyssen Ltd [**www.peternyssen.com**]
and Parker's Dutch Bulbs [**www.dutchbulbs.co.uk**].

Fêtes, fairs and fun days

The village fête is a mainstay of the British summer, and for
excellent reason. It brings people together, is a great community activity, is fun both to organise and attend, and is
something everyone from nought to 90 can enjoy.

So holding a fête in aid of a local community project – such
as a village hall or a youth centre, or the renovation of a play
area – can be a fantastic project, if a lot of hard work.

CASE STUDY _____

Stephen Hardaker, chairman of the Thornton-in-Craven fête
Thornton- in-Craven, in North Yorkshire, holds a popular summer fête every year.

"In organising a fête the hardest part is getting people to become involved in planning and coming on a committee. Plenty will turn up on the day to help set up but few will give an evening up after work to discuss planning.

The big money raisers at our fête are the bar and the barbecue. We keep it simple, wine red & white, bottled lager, canned beer, cans of pop and squash for the toddlers. These are bought when good offers are available in the supermarkets.

Stalls like pottery smashing are good fundraisers as it is free to set up – charity shops are only too glad to offload the large amounts of unsaleable pottery they get given. Get someone who is handy at woodwork to make you some tennis ball-sized wooden balls.

We hired a ducking stool this year. It was great fun but only broke even on the hire cost due to the poor weather.

A greasy pole is another good idea, providing it gets past the 'health and safety police'.

You need a 12-in diameter drainage pipe 10ft-15ft long mounted on a tripod at either end. Two people sit astride this and try to knock each other off with pillows. Go to your local bed shop and ask for some old mattresses to put underneath for safety.

The Women's Institute do well at our fête by doing afternoon teas and cakes.

*Try not to have too many little stands as they all need man-
ning and people have only a certain amount to spend.*

*We involve the local school who get the children to produce
some kind of craft entry based on a topic they are covering at
school. This gets the interest of the parents so they come to the
fête."*

Ideas for stalls and games at a fête:

- Ball in bucket
- Bands and music
- Bash the rat
- Beat the buzzer
- Beat-the-goalie
- Bouncy castle
- Candy floss
- Coin tower or coin snake
- Coconut shy
- Cream teas
- Dance displays
- Dog show
- Donkeys – rides or a donkey derby, pin the tail on the
  donkey
- Face-painting
- Fishing pond/hook a duck
- Guessing games – guess the flavour of a sweet, number
  of sweets in a jar, weight of a cake, number of dog bis-
  cuits in a jar, number of balloons in a car, name of a doll
  or teddy, who's who in the baby photos
- Hoopla or horseshoe-throwing
- Ice creams

- Lucky dip
- Magic show
- Pick a lolly
- Pig roast
- Plant and bulb stall
- Putting green
- Races – egg and spoon race, three-legged, sack race, 'jelly welly' race
- Ring toss
- Roll a coin
- Rounders tournament
- Skittles
- Spud-lebrity – competition to decorate a potato to represent your favourite celebrity
- Story-telling corner
- Tombola
- Treasure hunt – draw a map of buried treasure and charge people for a guess
- Tug of war
- Wet sponge throwing
- Welly throwing competition

Top tip £££££££££££££££££££££££££££££££

Don't despise the obvious – tombolas and raffles are always popular, but vary things for interest. When collecting donations, ask people to give you one or two *small* things – a thimble, a nail brush, a jar of nail varnish, a little bag of sweets – then put a bran tub together with all of these little things. Or do a 'pink' tombola – takes a bit of organising but it's fun and looks different and nice. *Susan Hill*

Setting it up

- Think about how you price your tickets – don't overcharge if the majority of your prizes are quite low in value.

- The winning numbers are usually those that end in 0 or 5.

- Alternatively, party supply companies such as Peeks [www.peeks.co.uk] sell pre-printed tombola draw tickets which state whether you have won a prize or not.

- If it takes place on private property and the tickets are sold and results declared at the event itself, you will not need a licence for your tombola. But if it's in a public place you might, so contact your council to find out if this is the case.

Some ideas for themed tombolas and bran tubs:

- Boys only
- Pink or another colour
- Food and drink
- Chocolate
- Animals – good for children
- Adults only

Gift Clearance [www.giftclearance.com] supply end of line items at big discounts, so check if there are suitable items for sales and tombolas.

Seasonal events

Hanging your event on the 'hook' of a holiday or calendar day means that you have a ready-made starting point for ideas.

It can also make publicising your event easier as local media may well be looking for stories related to these days, and members of the public could well already be looking for something to do or go to, to mark the day or a way to spend a bank holiday.

Here are some seasonal events and a few ideas that might get your fundraising imagination working.

Month	Day	Ideas and inspirations
January	Burns Night	A piper, a whisky-bearer, The Selkirk Grace, Haggis, Scottish quiz, neeps and tatties, Robert Burns readings (including the Address to a Haggis), Scottish songs, Auld Lang Syne.
February	Valentine's Day	A 'famous couple' fancy dress competition, a love-themed quiz, heart-shaped biscuits and cakes, A Romance Raffle, a sponsored slow dance, a marathon of love songs, a sponsored kiss, an anti-Valentine's Day party, love-grams or send-a-flower (this works well within schools and colleges).
	Shrove Tuesday	Pancake race – vary it for interest with different heats. You could include a relay race and an obstacle course. Pancake tossing competition, pancake stall, pancake eating competition.
	Chinese New Year	Dim sum, Fortune cookies, calligraphy, traditional dress – cheongsams and Chinese masks, Chinese food stands, animal of the Chinese calendar for that year, traditional Chinese music and dance.

March	St David's Day	Cawl (leek broth), daffodil walk, Welsh quiz, Welsh language learning challenge, Welsh cakes, Dylan Thomas poetry reading
	St Patrick's Day	A 'green day', Irish dinner, champ, Irish jigs, Guinness, a treasure hunt leading to a pot of gold, corned beef and cabbage, a game of pin-the-hat-on-the-leprechaun, Irish stew, a ceilidh dance.
	Mother's Day	Mother's tea party or lunch, hand-made mother's day cards, spring bouquets.
	World Book Day	Book sale, sponsored read, story-telling tent, short story competition, design a bookmark competition and sell the winning design, literary quiz, dress as favourite literary character.
	No Smoking Day	Sponsored no-smoking.
April	Easter	Egg decorating competition, Easter egg hunt, egg and spoon race, breakfast/brunch party, hot cross bun sale or eating competition, rabbit pie dinner, egg rolling competition, Easter bonnet competition.
	April Fool's Day	Joke competition.
	Shakespeare's birthday	A sonnet writing competition; an Elizabethan banquet; a sponsored play-reading; a concert of Elizabethan music?
	St George's Day	a British quiz, a papier-mache dragon making challenge?

May	May Day	May Day garlands, May Queen, maypole dancing, morris dancing...
June	Solstice	Midsummer ball, performance of *A Midsummer Night's Dream*, midsummer picnic...
	Wimbledon	Tennis tournament, strawberries and cream Fortnight tea, tennis stars quiz, table tennis competition.
July	Bastille Day	Crêpes, cancan dancers, French picnic, French cheese and wine tasting, boules, coffee and croissants.
August	Notting Hill	Carnival, steel band, Caribbean food, limbo Carnival competition, calypso music.
September	Harvest Festival	Harvest feast, corn dollies, harvest loaves, produce show and sale.
October	Halloween	Ghost walk, ghost-story telling, haunted castles, most scary costume, pumpkin carving, horror film marathon, apple dunking.
	Diwali	Fireworks, candle sale, paper lanterns, henna hand-painting, diwali sweets.
November	Guy Fawkes Night	Bonfire party, toffee apples, guy competition, cinder toffee, sparklers, sausages.
	Thanksgiving	Thanksgiving dinner, sweet potato and pumpkin pie, roast turkey, cranberries.
December	Christmas	Carol concert, mulled wine, crib competition, Christmas cards, Christmas

pudding and cake sale, gift-wrapping
service, pantomime, wreaths, elves
and reindeers run, Christmas markets,
secret Santa (pay to take part),
mistletoe sprigs, donations in lieu of
Christmas cards, Father Christmas's
grotto, Christmas card delivery (limit
it to your local area and get people to
pay per card delivered).

Ideas to be wary of

Cookbooks. For a while these were the hot thing in fundraising, and it seemed like every community centre, school and church was printing a collection of local recipes, or children's favourite recipes, or family recipes. And although some still do well, they really need a big name attached to succeed. Most of them just aren't that interesting – food writing is a real art, and a badly written recipe can be a nightmare to make as well as uninspiring to read. They also require skill to compile and edit and aren't cheap to produce. And then there's the issue of illustrations – food photography is tricky to do well and expensive to print. In most cases, unless you have a really killer idea to make your collection stand out, or a celebrity chef prepared to commit to helping you, for example, you'd be better off looking elsewhere for an idea.

If you are set on the idea, the book *Will Write for Food* by Dianne Jacob contains lots of sound advice about recipe writing and self-publishing cookbooks.

Balloon launches. Although they sound like fun, these can cause damage to the environment and harm to wildlife. Some say there are ways of minimising any damage, but many feel they are not worth the risk.

Calendars. Although I've used this as an example of a successful Do it Yourself project, this very fact means that by the time you read this book, they may well have been done to death.

Part 2

Planning

Forming committees, delegating responsibilities and keeping organised

The most imaginative and innovative ideas for fundraising events will fall flat if they are not well planned and organised. You must keep on top of things and ensure that everyone involved is aware of their responsibilities and that there is someone who has a good overview of everything that is happening throughout the planning process.

A good way of helping you do this is to approach your fundraising like a small business. Keep records, minutes of meetings and receipts. Get some headed paper (it doesn't necessarily have to be expensively designed and you can do it on a word processor) – it will make your communications look much more professional. Set up a dedicated email address so that all messages are kept in one place, and again, it helps you look like an efficient and well-run organisation.

Forming a committee

This is the usual way to assign responsibilities and make sure everything gets done when organising some kinds of fundraising event, such as a large auction, a dinner-dance or a village fête.

If you have a target amount of money to raise and are planning on doing so with a number of smaller events, a committee is also an efficient way of keeping track of those events and how much money has been raised so far. This is how lots of church, community and student fundraising groups organise themselves.

CASE STUDY

Ben Ewan, Cambridge RAG President for 2006-2007, explains how the committee is set up for Cambridge RAG.

"It's crucial that there is never one person doing all the work since it ends up being entirely inefficient. We are still learning how to structure our committee but we realise the importance of having clearly defined roles. So we have a President who oversees the office and liaises with charities and so on. The Chair organises meetings, socials, makes sure the President is doing his job and keeps alumni up-to-date. Secretary is in charge of minutes, a college Treasurer oversees college accounts and a central Treasurer oversees the rest of the accounts.

We generally have someone appointed for each event we run; in Blind Date's case it is two. These are ultimately in charge of the event and coordinating things. However, the whole committee help out where they can.

We also have college reps who enable RAG to happen. Without them it would be impossible. They publicise each central event we run and sell tickets to their colleges. They also run their own events in college."

Some standard roles and their associated responsibilities are:

● **Chair.** Takes overall responsibility, is often the spokesperson if necessary, and oversees the management of the whole event. This is a big job and whoever takes it on will need to be extremely efficient, confident, organised and, most importantly, dedicated, to ensure that things go smoothly. They may be called upon to make difficult decisions on behalf of the group and to act as mediator in the case of disagreements, so they need to be self-assured and calm.

- **Vice-Chair** It is often a good idea to appoint a Vice-Chair, who can give the Chair general support, and take over at any meetings the Chair is unable to attend, for example. Having someone to fulfil this role is especially important when organising a large event.

- **Secretary.** The secretary will usually take minutes of meetings, type them up and distribute them afterwards, as well as take charge of general correspondence and letters of thanks after the event, and record keeping. Again, the Secretary needs to be organised and efficient. Someone with previous administrative or office secretarial experience, and who is familiar with word processing programs, would be ideal.

- **Treasurer.** Controls the money, both before the event (so dealing with any deposits and expenses, for example) and afterwards (collecting and delivering the money raised). The treasurer needs to be comfortable working with figures. An ability to use spreadsheets or previous experience with book-keeping or accounting would be desirable.

- **Publicity/PR officer.** It can be a good idea to assign someone the specific task of promotion and public relations for your event. They would then be the one to write press releases, talk to journalists and distribute posters and flyers, for example. The best person for this job would be someone who is confident, good with words, good at talking to people and possibly with a background in either sales or PR.

Think carefully about who you ask to be on your committee – you do not want to be let down, or have to ask someone to step down further down the line. So it's important to make sure that anyone you ask is aware of:

- Exactly what their role will involve and
- How much time it is likely to take up.

Of course, it's up to you how you divide jobs up, and who takes on what. The important thing is that someone has overall responsibility for each area, and that everyone knows what they are meant to be doing.

Draw up a master list of jobs and mark the person in charge of that area next to it, and distribute the list to the committee.

Forming a committee can be one of the hardest parts of your planning as you're likely to be asking for a regular and significant time commitment over a period of months, as Sam Spreadbury, who organises the annual fête in Thornton-in-Craven, acknowledges.

"In organising a fête the hardest part is getting people to become involved in planning and coming on a committee," he says. "Plenty will turn up on the day to help set up but few will give an evening up after work to discuss planning."

How to get people involved

You might be lucky and already be part of a group that is planning on raising money together – a group of churchwardens who want to raise money for repairs to the old and decrepit roof of the chapel, for example. In this case, your committee is likely to exist already, and it will be a more simple matter of assigning tasks to individuals.

If this isn't the case, and you need to recruit people to help you in order to get your event off the ground, you have some more work ahead of you before you can really get going. Do try and get other people on board – planning a large (or even a relatively small) event alone is more than many people can mange.

Your enthusiasm for the cause is going to be critical in persuading people to give up valuable time to help plan and organise. You'll need to get them to feel as passionately about the need to raise money as you do yourself. There are likely to be people who feel just as strongly as you do and who are willing to help, so it's a matter of finding them.

Drawbacks

Committees are not without their drawbacks. They are time-consuming, and disagreements can often arise among members. Mohinder Dosanjh says this is one of the hardest things about organising fundraising activities, in her experience.

"Problems and challenges are mostly to do with people not agreeing among themselves and commitment to carry out the task they are given," she says. "We have to ensure that we understand what each individual likes doing and what he or she is good at. It is important to acknowledge everyone's contribution to make them feel appreciated and valued."

So, once you've got people to agree to take part, don't forget to thank your committee regularly and make sure any concerns they have are raised are dealt with at the earliest opportunity, so any problems are nipped in the bud.

Setting goals

It's a good idea to draw up a schedule outlining what you want to achieve by when. This will ensure your plans stay on track and any problems are likely to become apparent sooner rather than later. Breaking tasks down into manageable chunks also helps motivate people – a series of smaller goals to work towards feels more achievable than one large, vague job.

Top tip £££££££££££££££££££££££££££££££££

Work backwards from your event date. Decide when you need things to be done by and draw up the plan on a wall calendar or in a spreadsheet on the computer.

Keeping it all in one place means you can easily tick off jobs as they are done, and see what is left to arrange.

Budgeting

Whether it's as an individual or as part of a committee,

whenever you're fundraising you must make sure you budget properly. This means:

- Setting a target.

- Making sure you don't overspend when planning. As a rule
  of thumb, you should be aiming to make at least three
  times what you spend on the event. This means you must
  keep track of your expenditure so it doesn't eat into profits.

- Having a clear idea of what the expenses will be. This
  comes back to whether you have done enough research
  regarding the planning of the event. You need a comprehensive list of all the costs that will be involved, and
  whether you are going to have to pay for them in advance
  or whether you've managed to get them sponsored or per-
  suaded the supplier to donate them.

Checklist of possible expenses

- Administrative costs: phone calls, stationery, internet
  charges, postage

- Marketing and publicity materials: posters, flyers, cost of
  a blog or website, advertising

- Travel and transport expenses

- Venue/hall/marquee hire

- Food and wine

- Ticket design and printing

- Licences

- Insurance

- Thank you gifts/letters

- Speakers' or performers' fees

- Security

- Entertainment, equipment hire

Keeping track

Set up a system that makes sense to you – whether it is a table in a word processing document, a file with different sections, or a spreadsheet – and use it to keep track of your incomings and outgoings. You can also use this to keep track of suppliers' details.

Sample expenses chart for karaoke night

Item	Cost £	Supplier	Contact details	Other info
Karaoke machine hire	N/A donation from supplier	Ken's Kool Karaoke Kit	0771234 56789	Delivery 24th January

Planning checklist

The following list is not exhaustive but is intended as a checklist to make sure you have thought about some of the issues involved in planning a fundraising event.

Obviously, depending on the type of event you are proposing, some of the points will not apply to you and there may be other things you should think about. However, this should provide you with a good starting point for your own, tailored list.

- Do you need permission from the charity you are raising money for?

- Do you need an entertainment or alcohol licence, a permit to run a lottery or other permission from your local council, or the police? If in doubt – check. Your council should be your first port of call.

- When will your event be held?

- Is there enough time to plan your event?

- Is the date you have chosen going to clash with any other events happening in your area, or even nationally?

- If it's outdoors, have you considered any impact bad weather might have on your event and made contingency plans?

- How much are you planning to raise and is this achievable with the sort of event you are organising?

- Have you thought of all the expenses involved? Will there be enough money left over to make it worthwhile?

- Who will come to your event?

- How will they find out about it – through local media, word of mouth, or posters?

- Can you get these materials printed easily and cheaply enough?

- If you're reproducing any charity or business logos on your promotional materials, have you had these checked and approved?

- Where will you hold your event? Do you have permission, is it free, is it affordable? Is it big enough? Does it have everything you will need? Is it easily accessible? Is it safe? Does it have enough fire exits?

- Have you kept a record of suppliers?

- Have you got a schedule? Make sure you allow enough time for everything that you have planned.

- Have you got someone willing to look after the budget and money?

- Have you thought about first aid if you're holding a larger public event? (St John Ambulance will attend public events – find your local office at **www.sja.org.uk**)

- Are you familiar with food hygiene rules and guidelines if you are going to be serving food?

- Have you decided what food you will serve, what ingredients you will need and who will make it?

- What will you serve food on – do you have enough plates and glasses, for example?

- Do you have refrigeration and cooking facilities?

- If you're having a raffle or auction how are you going to get prizes? Have you got somewhere to store them before the event? How will they be delivered to the winners?

- Who will be in charge on the day?

- Do you have enough volunteers who are willing and able to help?

- Do they all have enough information about the cause they are helping to raise money for to tell people about it if asked?

- Have you given them specific jobs – for example, someone should be in charge of the press, someone should be in charge of greeting sponsors and celebrity guests, you may need people to serve drinks, collect tickets, hand out prizes, help clear up and so on.

- Have you got a list of emergency phone numbers to hand on the day, in case anything goes wrong? This might include contact details for suppliers, committee members, sponsors, local media attending, and your local council/police.

- Have you got a list of everything you will need to hand on the day? For example, pen and paper, calculator, a float of change, a cash box, identification badges, a mobile phone, first aid and emergency repair kits, a list of important numbers.

- Is there anything else you can do at your event to raise more money?

Celebrities

Celebrity involvement can help attract media attention and publicity to your event and cause. But remember that those in the public eye will receive requests for help extremely frequently, so do make sure you think carefully about who to approach and how to do so before launching in.

Contacting celebrities

Tracking down contact details for celebrities and writing to them can take a lot of time and effort. It is best to approach people by letter rather than trying to track down phone numbers – for one thing you are very unlikely to be able to get direct phone numbers and, if you do, it would be considered unduly intrusive to be phoned with a charity request by someone unknown. Most people find it much easier to craft a clear, nicely worded letter than it is to tell people about their cause and ask for their help on the phone. And remember that in the majority of cases, your first contact will be with the agent, who can then pass a letter on to their client.

Whatever you do, don't be tempted to leave it until the last minute and assume you'll be able to find someone to come and open your fête or give you signed photographs at the drop of a hat, or you'll be disappointed and potentially have a disaster on your hands.

So leave plenty of time to get in touch with people's representatives, allowing time for them to forward letters on to people who may be out of the country. Think in terms of months not weeks – there are a number of steps that will need to happen before you get someone who is willing to endorse your event.

Draw up your celebrity wish-list

Be realistic. Simon Cowell is extremely unlikely to agree to judge your school talent contest. Don't waste time and money approaching people who are hardly ever in the country, for example.

But also aim high. There's no harm in writing to a few people who are long shots, if there is a real reason why they might do it. For example, if there is a local link or the cause is one that you know they have particular sympathies with, it might be worth a go.

BRIGHT IDEA

While Simon Cowell might not come and judge your contest, he may donate some signed photographs that you can use as prizes, or even in your posters – you could put a photograph of him on a chair next to the other judges, and have him there 'in spirit'. Little touches like this can make your event fun and even help you get that all-important media attention, if you are clever about it.

Think links. Spend some time thinking about possible links – the more personal your appeal is to the celebrity, the more likely they are to be willing to participate. Are there any celebrities who live or were born in your local area? Try and match the celebrity to the event – a local golfer or footballer may be more likely to agree to referee a five-a-side football match than they are to judge a comedy night. Having said that, some celebrities get asked to do the same thing again and again, so try and think a bit laterally.

BRIGHT IDEA

Alternatively, think strategically about which celebrities might be right for your cause, however tenuous that association may be. An example of this might be an animal welfare charity approaching a TV vet or an actor who plays the role of a vet, or a health charity requesting the help of celebrity doctors or actors from television medical dramas. *The Celebrity Index*

This is where doing your research will really come in useful and pay dividends. Regional television and radio can be an excellent source of information and news stories which might give you ideas about people to approach. Also read your local county magazines to see who they're interviewing and featuring. Keep your eyes open to see who is doing book signings in your area. If you have a local theatre, see what's on and who is performing – actors in touring productions might be willing to get involved while they are in town. Remember, though, that they may only be in your area for a short time so check that the timings will work before approaching them.

As well as all of this, don't forget to look closer to home. Is there anyone on your committee or in your circle of contacts who might know people who'd be willing to help? Sometimes a friend of a friend or a business contact can provide great results, and an approach through someone you know can often be far more effective than 'cold calling'.

Top tips £££££££££££££££££££££££££££££££

Be aware of the possibility of negative publicity. While researching for a celebrity, look into their history – make sure none of this conflicts with your charity. Do look for ways a celebrity can generate publicity, but only for the right reasons.

Celebrities are approached all the time to endorse charities. Always do some research on the internet about celebrities and any background they may have with other charities that share the same cause. Check which celebrities are likely to be sympathetic to your cause and also whether they will appeal to your target audience.

Choosing the wrong celebrity can result in drawbacks and may ultimately do your cause more harm than good. Do lots of research. Inexperienced celebrities who are not sympathetic to your cause can deter audiences and even attract bad publicity. They should be motivated into joining the cause. Remember, they may be asked to conduct a press conference or appear in public on behalf of a charity, so they need to conduct themselves in an appropriate manner, too. *The Red Pages*

Find addresses and contact details

The Celebrity Index. This is an online, searchable database of celebrity contact details, which was founded by an ex-corporate fundraiser. It includes features such as a comprehensive list of regional presenters and contact details for all major football, cricket and rugby clubs in Britain. You have to pay for it, but it's worth considering for the amount of time it might save you. **www.thecelebrityindex.co.uk**

The Red Pages. This is a subscription celebrity contacts service, and is used by hundreds of PR and fundraising professionals. As well as providing details for how to contact celebrities, it also contains information on celebrity birthplaces, celebrity interests and skills so you can match celebrities to events, as well as charity affiliations. If you think you're going to be contacting a large number of celebrities, it might well be worth investing in a subscription [020 7190 7788 **www.theredpages.co.uk**].

If you can't pay for the use of one of these resources, then you're going to have to track down contact details using a bit of ingenuity. Here are some good starting points.

Google. You never know, just putting someone's name into Google can often throw up the website of someone's agent, publicist or publisher. If it does, then your search is obviously over. If nothing comes back, or, possibly worse, you get seven million results and not one of them looks relevant, you're going to need to narrow things down.

Searching for name + agent, or name + publicist is worth a try. Still nothing? Then try these sites.

If you're looking for actors

The Internet Movie Database. This is a huge online database that lists details of films, actors and other film industry professionals. Some of the actors' pages have their agents' details listed. **www.imdb.com**

Spotlight. This is a book which is used by casting directors but can also be of real use when trying to track down the contact details for over 30,000 actors, presenters and other performers. You can search it online at **www.spotlight.com**

If you're looking for writers, or celebrities who've published a book

Publicity departments of publishers will often forward letters to their writers if you ask nicely. You can find the details on most major publishers' websites.

Talent agencies

Look on the websites of talent agencies, who will often list their clients. You can then write to the celebrities care of the agent. Try and write care of the individual who represents them, rather than just sending your letter to the main address.

Some talent agencies in the UK

19 Entertainment: 33 Ransomes Dock, 35-37 Parkgate Road, London SW11 4NP, Tel: 0 20 7801 1919, **www.19.co.uk**

Creative Artists Management: 1st Floor, 55-59 Shaftesbury Avenue, London W1D 6LD, Tel: 020 7292 0600, **www.cam.co.uk**

Hamilton Hodell: Fifth Floor, 66-68 Margaret Street, London W1W 8SR, Tel: 020 7636 1221 **www.hamiltonhoddell.co.uk**

ICM London: Oxford House, 76 Oxford Street, London, W1D 1BS, Tel: 020 7636 6565

John Noel Management: 2nd Floor, 10a Belmont Street, London NW1 8HH, Tel: 020 7428 8400

Peters, Fraser & Dunlop, Drury House, 34-43 Great Russell Street, London, WC2B 5HA, Tel: 0207 344 1000, **www.pfd.co.uk**

PBJ Management: 7 Soho Street, London, W1D 3DQ, Tel: 020 7287 1112, **www.pbjmgt.co.uk**

Sanctuary Artist Management: The Sanctuary Group plc, Sanctuary House, 45–53, Sinclair Road, London, W14 0NS, Tel: 020 7602 6351, **www.sanctuarygroup.com**

Vivienne Clore: The Richard Stone Partnership, 2 Henrietta Street, London, WC2E 8PS, Tel: 020 7497 0849

Please note that this is not a comprehensive list. A much fuller list of agents can be found in Contacts, published annually by The Spotlight and available from **www.spotlight.com/shop/contacts**. A full list of literary agents can be found in the Writers' and Artists' Yearbook, which is updated annually and published by A&C Black.

Draft your letter

Top tip £££££££££££££££££££££££££££££££

Celebrities' agents receive requests all the time, so ensure that your proposal is comprehensive and covers the level of involvement you'd like from the celebrity. You can contact celebrities through their own websites or their agent's site [see Red Pages **www.theredpages.co.uk**]. *The Red Pages*

Sample letter:

Your Name
Your Address
Date

Dear Famous Celebrity,

I am writing to ask if you might consider supporting the Small Groups Fundraising Event. *(Tell them what you're asking straight away – don't make them search for the information.)* This event will take place on X Date at X Location and will be a fun evening featuring delicious food, fine wine and jelly and ice-cream. *(Say what's going to happen. Make it sound as appealing as you can. If there's anything you can tailor to the celebrity's known interests or job, make sure you mention it)*

The event is in aid of Raising Big Money. This is a group of local people who are deeply committed to Raising Big Money and need all the support they can get as they work towards their goal of Raising Big Money. *(Who is it in aid of? Why do they deserve help? What will money raised go towards? Be specific.)*

Would you be able to come and present the prize for Most Money Raised at the evening? *(What are you asking them to do?)* You would be collected from the local train station, and would need to be present for at least two hours. All expenses would, of course, be paid. *(What are you asking them to do specifically?)* Alternatively, if you are not able to attend the evening, would you consider giving us a quote in support of the event that we can use in publicising it? *(Is there an alternative way they can help?)*

Your reputation as a supporter of Similar Events or Charity means we know you must get lots of requests for help of this kind *(Get in any links and acknowledge that they are constantly asked for help)* but any support you feel able to give us would be extremely valuable and very much appreciated.

We can be contacted at the above address or by telephone on 123456789 or email at email@fundraisisngevent.co.uk. *(If you have a deadline, politely mention it here.)*

Thank you very much for your time reading this and I hope to hear from you in due course.

Kind regards,

Hopeful Fundraiser

Report from the front line

The job of a celebrity PA involves sifting through hundreds of letters such as yours every year. Here, Jo Crocker, PA to Stephen Fry gives the inside scoop on what sends requests straight to the shredder, and what will get you one step closer to the celebrity you are targeting.

"Receiving many requests by letter for financial help both for local fund-raising activities and personal matters such as post-graduate degree fees, acting courses and the like has made it somewhat necessary to apply a few initial sifting strategies to the 50 to 70 letters that arrive in the office on average each month.

"A misspelt name and a general address 'To whom it may concern' is frankly not on and generally implies that the writer of the letter hasn't really bothered to come up with an appropriate list of those he or she wishes to target.

"A letter written on a single side of the page, with an opening paragraph that gets straight to the point of the 'big ask' is so much easier to absorb than pages of detail that very often repeats itself by the end. Gimmicks like DVDs or extra printed-out pages simply clutter up the desk and in the past have slightly irritated us when the money sought is to help with a green issue of one kind or another.

"Getting to the point of what's wanted really is important. Very often the writer will say something along the lines of "any amount, no matter how large or small will help". It may be true, but it is also confusing. Is £10 really going to make a difference or is the writer really hinting at £1,000? I particularly like the tactic often used by students and individuals (rather than organisations) when saying that the writer has "chosen 200 of his favourite/actors/writers/film directors to approach and if each one were to give £10/£30/£50 then the target for (whatever) will be reached.

"Conversely, a letter that helpfully tells you that the writer has written to and heard back from Bill Clinton, Bob Flowerdew, Kate Moss and others leaves one with the feeling of mild blackmail.

"However many people are on your list, try to personalise each letter where possible. Even if you know the recipient has no geographical connection with your part of the world where you are busily securing funds for your playgroup/church roof/donkey sanctuary – find one. Has the actor performed locally? Has the writer mentioned your town or village in a novel? Has the director filmed in your neck of the woods? Little things like that stand out. Mad drawings and stickers simply don't."

Then you just have to wait

Be prepared for it to take some time for people to reply.

> **Top tip** ££££££££££££££££££££££££££££££££
>
> After your initial approach, don't badger or pester the celebrity's agent for a reply. They will respond in good time. A sure-fire way to reduce your chance of success is to fall foul of the celebrity's gatekeeper – the agent. *The Celebrity Index*

Also, accept that a lot of people just won't respond. A response rate of approximately 10% is probably a reasonable one to expect.

When deciding how many celebrities you may need to approach to get a positive response, The Red Pages points out: "You will need to be realistic about the size of your charity and the celebrity you want affiliated to your cause. A-list celebrities have incredibly hectic schedules while lesser-known celebs are more inclined to attend/speak at charity events. So if you're looking to attract a big celebrity, then you may need to target a lot more than you would a lesser-known face. It'll be easier to scan newspapers for stories on personal causes celebrities may mention in interviews and biographies."

But remember not all of those will be positive ones – many may be refusing for all sorts of reasons. Don't let this disappoint you, people are very busy and simply can't accept every request they receive.

What to do if you don't get any positive responses

If you draw a blank, it could be time to rethink your strategy.

Some possible problems might be:

- Are you writing to the right people? Maybe you need to rethink your wish list.

- Is your letter punchy enough? Does it get straight to the point? Could it be putting people off?

- Could it be that your event is the problem? Maybe it's going to take people too long to travel to it, or it's just not unusual enough.

When you are successful

You can see there's an assumption in the title of this – that you *will* be successful. Have faith! You will get there in the end, as long as you have planned your approach carefully and left yourself enough time.

So, let's say you now have a celebrity who is willing to attend your event, as well as quotes from a couple of others in support of it. And maybe even a couple of pieces of memorabilia as well.

What are the key things to remember?

Top tip £££££££££££££££££££££££££££££££££££

Be sure to confirm *in writing* exactly what it is you require from them, whether it be a speech at a campaign launch, a personal appearance at a fundraising event, or permission to use their name and image on your fundraising materials.

Feel free to invite the celebrity to view your work for themselves. This will give you an opportunity to introduce yourself in person, fire their enthusiasm for your cause, go over the details of any requirements you may have of them and help sow the seeds of a fruitful partnership.

NB: It is often expected that an organisation should provide basic expenses associated with a celebrity's attendance at an event or function. These include taxi fares and refreshments, within reason! It is probably best to agree in advance what is and, more importantly, what is not covered by your expenses.
The Celebrity Index

BRIGHT IDEA

If the celebrity agrees to visit, you might be able to use this for publicity by inviting the local media along, or photographing their visit to use in future promotional material. You should always ask permission first.

If the celebrity is attending an event, rather than lending their name or donating items, then make sure you arrange their attendance carefully so it all runs smoothly. Nominate someone to collect them, or if that is not practical, to be waiting for them when they arrive, greet them, and generally be in charge of making sure they have everything they need and deal with any last-minute problems or issues that might arise.

Saying thank you

It is really important to make sure you thank people who've

helped you. Offer them a visit to come and see the hospice you're fund-raising for, for example, or send them one of the calendars you've put together to raise money. It doesn't matter what you offer them, but people appreciate the thought.

Top tip £££££££££££££££££££££££££££££

If they're local offer a home-made cake or some jam to be taken round once they've done something for you; it's cheaper than flowers, and more personal.

I recently received a lovely CD of a school singing songs to thank me for giving some signed books. Some other children made me a dough wreath of flowers with 'Thank You' baked on.

It doesn't have to be much – you could make them an honorary member of your society or give them a similar title and get someone to make a certificate with calligraphy saying this.

It's all saying 'Thank You' without it costing a lot. You would be amazed at the number of signed books and other things I send out and for which I get not a jot of thanks. *Susan Hill*

BRIGHT IDEA

Think of other interesting or unusual ways to say thanks to those who have helped you, celebrities or otherwise. A collage, a photograph, a home-made card, a photo-journal style 'story of the day' could all be starting points for ideas.

Businesses and other sponsors

Fundraising costs money. From printing costs for promotional posters to day-to-day running expenses and deposits for venues, there are a number of costs involved in planning any event, and the fact that it's for charity does not mean you can afford to ignore these. Support from businesses can be invaluable in helping you lower your risk and maximise your profits.

Top tip ££££££££££££££££££££££££££££££££

I'd say that the most important thing to gain bigger donations is to get the commitment of a major employer involved to help out, particularly with any costs.

In the case of our T Day charity, that's supported by the Chelsea Building Society who provide most of the printing but we also have a committee that, as well as having members of the children's charities we support, also comprises members of a large solicitor's practice, the county council, Cheltenham Town FC, the local radio station, Mitsubishi Motors, and, um ... me!

We then use the skills and clout of these organisations to further the aims of the appeal so that, for example, the council encourages schools to participate as well as their own employees, the radio station actively promotes the charity, the football club donate their proceeds from the Charity Shield final in addition to providing match day sponsorship, programme info, and players for various photo calls. *Dale, from Gloucester Rugby Club*

When approaching businesses, whether you're asking for financial support, support in kind (giving their services for nothing, or products for raffle prizes, for example) or some other kind of help – like letting you advertise in a shop window – it's important to remember that they will receive many such requests.

Make a list

Again, start by making a list of everyone you know who you might be able to approach. Any of your friends or colleagues who are business owners would be a good place to start. Think of shops that you frequent regularly, where the proprietor knows you – your hairdresser, sandwich shop, or book shop, for example, might be more likely to offer their support if you have a personal connection with them.

Top tip ££££££££££££££££££££££££££££

The Goodwill Gallery [**www.goodwillgallery.co.uk**] provides a list of professionals and businesses offering their services to charities for free. It includes journalists, bookkeepers, designers, accountants, administrators and website builders, among others, so check to see if someone is offering the very service you need.

If you have thought about this in advance, when forming your committee, you may already have some local business people on board. Use them.

BRIGHT IDEA ☀️

If you are fundraising on behalf of an existing charity, contact them first. They are likely to have contacts with larger companies and so encourage you not to approach them but focus your attention on local businesses. They may also have contacts that you can use to get started.

Start close to home ...

... with your own place of work and those of your committee or volunteers. Some companies, especially larger ones, will offer to match money raised in return for some publicity on your flyers, for example.

There may also be existing links and contacts with suppliers or clients that you can utilise through your place of work.

Think laterally

Don't just think of the obvious and go to the same people every time. Apart from anything else, they are likely to be inundated with requests and simply unable to give to every one of them. Think of people who might be willing and able to help in an unusual way.

BRIGHT IDEA ☀️

Some companies (record companies and cosmetics, for example) get hundreds of requests from fundraisers but others don't. Not many screwdriver manufacturers will get many requests for free merchan-

dise, but think how useful they could be to you. You could put together a DIY hamper to give away as a prize, or a DIY-themed stall at a sale. Make a list of similar utilitarian firms in your area. Thinking sideways like this has netted me some great things in the past, but remember – ask nicely, don't assume, and offer to collect.
Susan Hill

Think links

Try and think of any links that you can make between the company you are approaching and your fundraising project. An optician's would be more likely to get involved with a project to raise money for a local school or group for blind children than a garden centre – but the garden centre may well be keen to help with a project that is going to take inner-city children to learn about nature.

Any links with the company's existing interests will be more likely to net you their interest in your project.

Other organisations to consider approaching

- Your local mayor – they often have their own charities and may offer their support to your appeal in some way.

- Rotary or Freemasons, or other similar organisations. They are often involved in fundraising of their own but may provide useful support and contacts.

- Your local Chamber of Commerce [**www.chamberonline.co.uk**].

Write your letter

As with approaching celebrities, you need to get across what you're asking for and why in a way that is concise, clear and above all, polite. Similar principles for letter writing apply – see the chapter on approaching celebrities for more on this.

Think about who you're writing to and tailor it accordingly. You would write a different style of letter to a large corporation, who you are asking to help you financially with publicity costs, than you would to a shop owner who you are asking to donate some of their stock, for example. But whoever you are writing to, make sure you are polite and respectful.

Keep it brief – as with most letters and press releases, one side of paper is preferable.

Do your research

You must target your letters if writing 'cold', otherwise you will be extremely unlikely to have any success with your efforts.

Write to an individual. Your letter may well go straight into the bin if you don't. Find out the name of an appropriate individual at the company and write to them.

Also do a bit of research into the company. Do they already support a fundraising project very similar to your own, for example? If so, they are unlikely to be interested in getting involved with yours as well. Or they may have specific policies on the types of things they will and won't support. Find out about these before you waste your time writing to them.

Consider including a flyer or something with a photograph or image with your letter. Josette Falzon says of her fundraising efforts in aid of the Cystic Fibrosis Trust: "I've had sponsorships and support from big companies. I had sent out a letter with a good flyer and response was good considering we come from a small country."

CASE STUDY

Mohinder Dosanjh, the chair of Trinjan Women's Social and Community Group in London, says that they always try and approach potential business sponsors through an existing contact. But when this isn't possible, and you're approaching people 'cold', make sure you state what you've already achieved.

Mohinder adds: "If we don't know anyone from a company we write to them for support about two months in advance. We always list our achievements, such as how much money we have raised so far and how we have been helping the local community. Since winning the GlaxoSmithKline health award we always mention it in our communication/promotional material to show that we are a credible organisation."

She also gives her tips for networking: "New groups need to get in touch with their local voluntary sector forum to register with them. There are always free training courses offered to trustees and volunteers from many voluntary organisations. We find these courses very useful for networking as well as learning. There are workshops/conferences organised locally where you meet potential funders. It is also very useful to get to know your local voluntary organisations. You can do joint projects with them and bid for joint funding."

Approach it like a business

The point above about networking is an important one. Businessmen and women use networking as a way of making and maintaining contacts that have the potential to help them further their aims, and you should do the same when fundraising. If you go about things in a professional manner, you are far more likely to be successful.

And when approaching businesspeople they will probably respond much more positively if it is done in a way that says you are an efficiently run organisation with whom an association would be beneficial – *to them* as well as to you.

What are you asking for?

Don't be too general and ask for vague 'support' – people won't be sure what they're being asked for and so will be unwilling to commit. Ask for specific help. Perhaps you are asking them to donate the printing of your publicity material so make sure you say exactly what you anticipate that will be (100 posters that you have already designed, and 200 flyers, for example).

This way they know exactly what they are being asked to commit to giving, and, if they say yes, both parties know where they stand from the beginning.

If you're asking for financial donations, say what that money will do. "I'm writing to ask if you will donate £100, which will pay for one bean bag for the sensory room for special needs children who we are supporting through fundraising. The bean bags provide soft, comfortable seating with no sharp edges." This is a lot more effective than simply asking for the money, without explaining where it will go.

When do you need it by?

Make sure this is clear as well, not least so that you have a deadline which will help you with your planning. If they haven't responded by that time, you can target other companies instead.

What are you offering them?

Always offer something in return. Exactly what this is may well depend on your event, your fundraising project and the company or business, but some ideas to get you started are:

- Their name, logo or other company information on posters, in brochures, wearing their T-shirt during your marathon run or their name on a website or in some other piece of promotion.

- Free tickets to your event for them and some of their clients, with the promise of an introduction to any celebrities who are attending.

- Photographs of their representative at your event, with the celebrity or handing over their company donation, which they can use in their own promotional material.

- Naming rights – part of an event, or a prize named after them.

- Use of their venue for a press launch or another event which could help raise their profile.

- Samples of their products provided at your event.

Follow-up phone call

It's worth following up your letter with a polite phone call. This can be a help to anyone who may have intended to respond but who hasn't got round to doing so. They can also ask any questions they may have and then, hopefully, agree to support you.

Say thank you

Put one member of your team or committee in charge of making sure that everyone who has helped you, whether it's with a small prize for a tombola or by taking on your venue hire costs, for example, is thanked in an appropriate and timely fashion.

A small gift for sponsors and donors is a nice gesture – it doesn't have to be expensive. See the chapter on *Celebrities* for some ideas of how to do this.

Also, see the chapters on *Celebrities* and sections on *Major missions* and *Grand events* for more tips and thoughts on approaching business and corporations for sponsorship and support.

Publicity and media

Getting publicity for your event is important for several reasons. You need to make sure people turn up at the right place and the right time, you want to raise the profile of your cause and pave the way for any future fundraising efforts, and you want to increase the amount of money raised for your cause or project overall, not just from your event. The media – newspapers, magazines, radio and television – can be a great way of achieving all of these things if you make your plans in good time and go about things in a way that will spike their interest.

Do be aware that the media have their own agenda. They want a story and if you can give it to them, you are more likely to get the coverage you are after. They are not a free publicity machine there for your benefit, so don't assume that they will be interested in your event just because it is for charity.

Make a plan

- Make a list of local papers, magazines and radio stations in your area.

How to find them

Local newspapers:
Find your local newspaper contact details from The Newspaper Society **www.newspapersoc.org.uk**
National daily newspaper websites and newsdesk email contacts:

The Times – **www.timesonline.co.uk**

    Home News – **home.news@thetimes.co.uk**

The Daily Telegraph – **www.telegraph.co.uk**

The Independent – **www.independent.co.uk**

    Newsdesk – **newseditor@independent.co.uk**

The Guardian – **www.guardian.co.uk**

    Newsdesk – **national@guardian.co.uk**

The Daily Mail – **www.dailymail.co.uk**

    News and features – **news@dailymail.co.uk**

Daily Express – **www.express.co.uk**

    Newsdesk – **news.desk@express.co.uk**

The Sun – **www.thesun.co.uk**

    Newsdesk – **news@the-sun.co.uk**

The Mirror – **www.mirror.co.uk**

    Newsdesk – **mirrornews@mirror.co.uk**

Local radio

You can find your local BBC radio stations on their website – go to www.bbc.co.uk and find your region.

You can search for independent local radio stations on **www.radio-now.co.uk**.

Local television

One website – www.itvlocal.com – brings the regional ITV stations together and provides contact details.

You can find local BBC stations on the main website.

Also look for any websites that are either local, linked to your charity or cause or have another link that you might be able to exploit. Keep your eyes open all the time for publicity opportunities – they can crop up in the strangest of places.

Finding named contacts

It's often best to contact a specific reporter. One way to find out this information is to note the bylines in the relevant publication.

There are also various public relations databases and directories which give you precise named contact details for all national, regional, local and trade media. They're very expensive to subscribe to but you may find a local business that already subscribes. Ask them to donate half an hour or so of their PR's time digging out the contacts you need.

If you're part of a group, assign someone the job of press officer. They'll be the main contact for the media throughout your fundraising process. Keep a note of all the names and contact details of people you get in touch with, and any interest they express.

When approaching journalists, remember to be polite, friendly and make sure they have all the information they need.

Top tips £££££££££££££££££££££££££££££

Sarah Foster, women's editor of The Northern Echo, one of the largest regional newspapers, has the following advice.

- In these computer-dominated days, the best way of contacting newspapers is by email.

- Do your homework to find out who the best person is or which is the best office to get in touch with. For example, if it's The Northern Echo and you're based in Durham, it's best to contact the Durham office.

- Be as imaginative as you can with ideas for pictures and quirky lines that can be featured in a story. Is there anything unusual about you or the cause you're promoting? If so, flag it up.

- Don't go mad with information. A press release of no more than a page should suffice, but do make sure you include contact details.

- Make sure you give enough advance notice of a forthcoming event. A week or so should be about right.

The best way of getting contacts for The Northern Echo is via the website [www.thenorthernecho.co.uk] and this is true for many regional newspapers.

The standard way of telling the press about forthcoming events and stories that might be of interest to them is with a press release. This is a simple document, usually on one side of paper, which outlines what the story is, gives a bit of background information and provides contact details.

Photographs

If you are submitting a story after the event, or the press are unable to attend themselves, you will probably find they are much more likely to run your story if you can supply them with a great photograph to accompany it. You may find a local photographer willing to cover your event for free, in return for the publicity it will bring them if their photographs are used. Perhaps there is college nearby that runs photography classes. A talented student might want to build up their portfolio by taking photographs for you. Be creative about it – someone in a suit shaking hands as they present a cheque = boring. Pictures involving kids, silly costumes, action shots and anything eye-catching and attention-grabbing are far more likely to help get your story printed.

The Association of Photographers' website [**www.the-aop.org**] provides a database of members, searchable by specialism.

Top tips ££££££££££££££££££££££££££££

Consumer public relations specialist Claire Park has worked on a number of high profile campaigns across various sectors and for charities such as Leukaemia Research, The Salvation Army and the British Heart Foundation. She says that the key things to remember when writing a press release are:

- **Keep it concise.** Press releases don't have to be long and complicated, in fact, the shorter and more concise the better. Press releases should keep to the point, be well-written and, most importantly, newsworthy. Consider how interesting the story really is – if it's an event or new campaign, the chances are that it is interesting.

- **Keep it clear.** Press releases should ideally follow the following format:
  - Headline
  - Lead paragraph – the most important paragraph in the whole release this should cover the who, what, where, when, why and how of the story
  - Quote – consider including a quote from a key person involved in the activity

- Contact details – provide as many contact details (phone/ mobile/ email/ website) to make it as easy for the media as possible.

- **Keep it local.** If your story has a local angle make sure that you highlight it.

- **Make it quotable.** The media like to quote statistics, facts or figures. If you're hoping to raise £1m in six months, then say so.

- **Make it timely.** Issue the press release to the media in good time
  - If you're publicising an event before it takes place, ensure that you let the media know well in advance as they may wish to attend or send a photographer.

If you're issuing a story about an event that has already happened, make sure you do so as soon as possible afterwards. A week or two later on simply isn't news.

Sample press release

Local chef cooks up a storm for meals on wheels

(Fun and snappy title, says who you are and what you're doing straight away.)

John Brown, head chef at Cook It Up Restaurant on Bakers Lane, is holding a sponsored cook-off at 2pm on Thursday 13th December to raise money for the new Meals on Wheels service.

The cook-off will put him head to head with four other chefs from the area, each of whom will have to create their 'signature dish'

in a set amount of time and on a limited budget of just 75 pence
a head. The results will then be judged by a panel comprising
some of the residents from the home who will benefit from the
mobile catering service, which is scheduled to start serving up
tasty, nutritious meals to 100 local residents in the New Year.

(Says exactly what the event is and who it's going to benefit.
Statistics or facts and figures are easily quotable by journalists.)

"I wanted to use my skills as a chef to give something back to
the community that has given me so much" says John, who was
nursed back to health following a near-fatal accident at the Feel
Better Soon Clinic. "The Meals on Wheels service is long overdue
– for years some of our neighbours have struggled to feed themselves because of a lack of transport and limited funds. This is
the first time such a service has been run for over ten years, and
our opportunity to make sure they get at least one hot, healthy
meal a day."

(A quote gives press something to use in their piece, as well as
making it more personal. Don't be afraid to include any emotive
or dramatic details that make a story jump out. If your event is a
first or in some other way particularly noteworthy, again, say so.)

Money raised at the event will go towards buying a new van to
transport the meals and paying towards the running costs of the
scheme.

(States exactly what the money is going towards – be as specific
as you can.)

Press are welcome to attend. For more details or to make a donation contact John on 123456789 or by email at
johnthechef@email.com

Media management

Dealing with the media can be unnerving if you're not used to it – even seasoned celebrities get nervous sometimes. But with some simple tips you can ensure you keep calm and present yourself and your charity to their best advantage.

Before rushing in front of the TV cameras, however, have a think about who the best person is to be spokesperson. If you're part of a committee, nominate someone for this role once you've made sure they are happy to take it on. It might not be the chair or the brains behind the idea – whoever you choose should be confident, calm, comfortable being inter-viewed and able to talk up your cause with passion and enthusiasm. Picking the right person to do this is half the battle.

Once you've done that, the following guidelines should help you plan your media campaign.

Preparing for interviews

- Relax! And remember they're not trying to catch you out.

- Ask how long the interview will be so you have an idea of how much detail you'll be required to go into.

- Make some notes on any particular points you want to make. Also, jot down some key facts about both your event and the charity – it's very easy to forget things when you're on the spot.

- Don't just rely on facts and figures. If it's in advance of the event, think of something quirky you have planned and try to make sure it gets mentioned so as to get people's attention.

- If the interview is to take place after the event, think of an anecdote from the event or an interesting description that you can use to bring it to life in people's imaginations.

- Think about where the interview is going to be printed or aired and tailor your responses accordingly.

- Speak slowly and clearly – try not to gabble or swallow your words.

- Try not to 'um' and 'ah'.

- Use straightforward language, not specialist terminology or jargon.

- Enjoy it!

On the day

If you've succeeded in getting journalists to come to your event, make sure someone is in charge of greeting them and ensuring they have everything they need. Offer them a drink, make sure they can find the people they need to talk to easily, that they have clear access to any photo opportunities, and that they have the key information about the event. Prepare a sheet that they can take away with them giving the names and details that they may need to write their article.

Follow up

After the event, give them a call or send them an email to make sure they have everything they need, thank them for coming, and tell them about anything else that happened that they may have missed.

Other forms of publicity

Leaflets, posters and flyers. A nicely compiled leaflet or flyer, with an eye-catching image, can be invaluable when promoting your event.

If you or someone you know has a PC and a digital camera, you can put something together easily and cheaply. If you're raising money for a local cause, consider including a photograph of it – the church in need of repair or the hospital in need of a piece of equipment, for example. Seeing where the money is going to go can bring home the need for it. Remember to include any logo for the charity as well.

Otherwise you can use a photograph or image related to the event. Make sure you use simple, bold images and include all the necessary information, but don't clutter the page with lots of text.

Get a group of volunteers together to help you distribute leaflets and ask local shops, churches, school and community centres if you can display your promotional material in their windows or on notice boards.

Trinjan, a women's social and community group, use flyers to publicise their fundraising in various ways.

- Give to families, friends and colleagues and ask them to display them in their places of work.

- Send them to their local council magazine.

- Distribute them via local libraries and a newsletter for the voluntary sector in their area.

What other avenues might you be able to explore to distribute your leaflets?

Window displays. Another way for local businesses to get involved is to ask them to create displays in their shop windows, related to the event or charity. You could even make it into a competition, with a prize presentation at the event itself for the most eye-catching display. Ask your mayor or another community official to judge it, perhaps?

Word of mouth. This is far-reaching, with the potential to engage people emotionally and get them backing your cause long-term as well as donating money – and best of all, it's free.

There really is no substitute for good, old-fashioned enthusiasm. Talk to all of your friends, family and colleagues and tell them what you're doing and why. If you're organising a fête or quiz night, or similar ticketed event, have a supply of leaflets on hand at all times to give to anyone who might be interested in attending. If you're participating in a sponsored event, have plenty of spare forms and give one to anyone willing to help. Widening your circle like this is a really important part of raising money.

Remember that you're trying to raise general awareness for your cause as well as getting people to donate cash. Tell people why the cause deserves their support – you might even inspire others to organise their own fundraising events.

CASE STUDY

Josette Falzon has raised more than £60,000 for the Cystic Fybrosis Trust with a wide variety of events. She and her fellow fundraisers have used all means possible to raise their profile and she says there is no substitute for being able to communicate your passion for the cause.

As a main resource, we used TV & newspaper coverage, she says. I must say that when children are involved people are more generous. You just have to be prepared to be open about the situation.

I'm lucky in that one of Malta's top journalists is a very good friend of mine and she was the first to get our story in Malta's leading newspaper. We then got other newspapers and TV stations calling for an interview.

Regarding getting attention for events, I usually send out an email to all on my address book and ask for people to pass round. We also get a press release in newspapers, but it's word of mouth that has probably worked the best.

The internet, blogs and email. You can't afford not to use the internet when fundraising – it's a resource that makes research much easier and quicker, but perhaps even more importantly, it's a way of reaching potentially millions of people. And there is a variety of different ways of using it to your best advantage. It all depends on what you're trying to do and what you have available in the way of time and resources.

Email. This is one of the simplest ways of using the internet. Sending an email about your event has one major advantage over a letter – it's free. However, bear in mind that not everyone has email and so you should consider preparing a 'snail mail' letter as well. Also, it can be easy (and appropriate in some cases) to use very casual language in emails, but when you're sending emails that are requests for donations or other forms of support you should keep the tone polite, friendly and professional.

Adding a link to your website or Justgiving page that automatically appears at the bottom of every email you send can be an effort-free way of telling and reminding people you're in contact with what you're doing.

Remember, if you intend using a work email address you should ask your employer's permission before you do so.

Blogs. Blogs are either free or cheap both to set up and maintain. You also don't need specialist computer knowledge to do so as most of them have pre-loaded templates that you can simply customise according to how you want it to look. You can keep a diary to let your supporters know of your progress, you can include photographs and include links to Justgiving or other ways of donating money.

Top tip ££££££££££££££££££££££££££££££

Tamryn Kirby, who participated in the MoonWalk in aid of breast cancer charities, found a blog invaluable. Setting up a blog meant that whenever people searched for 'MoonWalk' we came up quite high, she says. This got a lot more sponsorship as well and helped drum up lots of support.

Websites. It's more expensive to construct a website than it is to set up a blog and needs considerably more technical knowledge. But if you know a website designer who might be prepared to donate some of the time, or you can get a website design company to construct a site for you in return for putting their logo on it, for example, it could allow you greater flexibility to create a visually exciting and interactive space for your online fundraising.

BRIGHT IDEA

Team Mongolian Job kept a regularly updated list of equipment and supplies that they were in need of on their website, ticking items off as people donated them.

If you can do this, then great. If you can't persuade someone to do it for you, and you don't know your HTML from your CSS, then it's probably safer to stick with a blog, or at least a very simple site – an amateurish and badly put together website with out of date links or a difficult to navigate design could do more harm than good in promoting your cause.

See the section on Justgiving under 'Sponsored events'.

These are just some of the main ways the internet can help

you reach your target, but with so many millions of websites out there, the opportunities are almost limitless.

Ben Fillmore made an expedition to Everest Base Camp in aid of The Stroke Association. Instead of simply relying on sponsorship for this expedition to raise his target amount of money, he came up with an unusual stunt that netted him attention from the national and international media, as well as topping up his coffers. He did this using eBay, the internet auction site [**www.ebay.co.uk**].

CASE STUDY

Ben Fillmore on raising awareness as well as money

Getting mass publicity is one of the best ways to help your chosen charity. I don't feel like it's just the financial side of things that you have to worry about. I recently managed to get onto prime time Saturday evening news in London on the BBC, ITV and Sky by doing a stunt that cost me 35 pence. It also hit local and national press, global news websites and even the Washington Times.

The secret? eBay is a great publicity tool and if you auction something original and kooky for charity the press lap it up. I decided to offer my face for a public fish-slapping inspired by the great Monty Python sketch.

The auction closed at £210, I received about £150 in side donations and a weekly magazine called Pick Me Up (with a circulation of 445,000) bought the story for £150. A huge number of people have read the story and so seen the name of my chosen charity. I saw the media coverage report for my charity for that week and my stunt accounted for 100% of

their broadcast coverage and about 75% of their local press / radio coverage.

In addition, companies are now interested in sponsoring me because of the publicity I am getting, which in turn is creating more funds for the charity. I've made a huge number of contacts who are now interested in hearing about my next stunt.

Rules and regulations

There are strict and complex laws and rules surrounding some aspects of fundraising and running events that you should be aware of. In many cases they may not apply to you but make sure you double check anything you are at all unsure about.

As a general rule of thumb, if in doubt, get in touch with your local council first – they may be the right people to deal with your query and if they're not they can usually point you in the right direction.

Setting up a charity

Setting up a new charity is not always the best way to go about things. It depends on what you are trying to achieve and how. For example, you cannot set up as a charity if you are fundraising for a specific individual who perhaps has an illness or disability. You can, however, establish a non-charitable trust fund for their benefit, or join forces with an existing charity working to help others with their condition.

The Charity Commission is the regulatory body in England and Wales and the place to find all the information that you need on this. They maintain a detailed online 'knowledge base' that explains the law regarding charities at www.charitycommission.gov.uk. Alternatively, you can contact them at Charity Commission Direct, PO Box 1227, Liverpool, L69 3UG, or on 0845 3000 218.

Street collections

You will need a permit or licence from your local authority if you want either to collect money or to sell on the street and in public places, and they are normally only given to registered charities. If you're in London, you should contact the police or the Common Council of the City of London.

Lotteries

Essentially, a lottery is considered to be a 'distribution of prizes by chance' where participants buy a ticket in return for the chance of winning a prize.

Lotteries are divided into three categories: private lotteries, small lotteries and society lotteries. If you are holding a raffle, perhaps as part of a larger event, it is likely that this will be classed as a small lottery and you will not have to register it or take any further action.

Private lotteries can only be held by and for a defined group of people. They must all either live or work on the same premises, or they must all belong to a single organisation that has not been set up for the purposes of gaming. Although it doesn't have to be registered, a private lottery can not be advertised outside the relevant premises (and on the tickets) and it must only be promoted by a member who has written permission from the governing body of the organisation.

All tickets must be the same price, which must be on the ticket, as must the name and address of the promoter and a statement that sales are restricted and who is eligible to buy them. Tickets cannot be sent through the post. Refunds can't be given, and all the proceeds of the lottery (after printing and stationery costs) must be used for prizes and/or the purposes of the society.

Small lotteries are frequently exempt from having to register with the Gambling Commission and are defined as a lottery which is incidental to an exempt entertainment. Exempt entertainments are things such as a fête, dinner, dance, sale of work, sporting or athletic event or bazaar.

Within this, there are some other conditions which must be observed:

- There can be no cash prizes.

- The tickets must be sold and issued and the results announced during the entertainment, and on the premises where the entertainment is being held.

- No more than £250 can be spent on buying prizes.

- There are no limits on the number of tickets sold, or the ticket price, nor are there age limits on either the buyers or sellers of tickets.

Society lotteries are promoted by or on behalf of a society (so a club or other organisation), which is established for charitable, sporting or cultural purposes, or other similar purposes with no aspect of private gain.

If the sale of lottery tickets will exceed £20,000 in value (or if taken together with sales from previous lotteries in the same year, will exceed £250,000) then it must be registered with the Gambling Commission.

If the sale of tickets is less than this, the charity must register with the local authority.

Either way, there are detailed regulations about how such lotteries must be conducted. The Gambling Commission produces a booklet called *Lotteries and the Law* to help societies and charities run a legal lottery. It covers things such as age restrictions, maximum ticket price (£2) and similar. This can be downloaded from the website at **www.gamblingcommission.gov.uk**, or you can telephone their helpline on 0121 230 6666.

Gambling Commission
4th Floor
Victoria Square House
Victoria Square
Birmingham
B2 4BP
Tel: 0121 230 6500
Fax: 0121 233 1096
Web: **www.gamblingcommission.gov.uk**

Licensing

The licensing laws are regulated by the Department for Culture, Media and Sport. The licensing laws changed in 2005 with the introduction of the Licensing Act 2003, so do make sure any information you may have already is up to date. Full information is available from the Charity Commission [**www.charity-commission.gov.uk**] and information specific to your local area from the DirectGov site [**www.direct.gov.uk**].

You will need a premises licence and designated supervisor if you are planning to sell alcohol at your event. Alternatively, many of the events mentioned in this book, or that you are likely to hold, will be eligible for a Temporary Event Notice. These allow you to conduct one or more licensable activity for no more than 96 hours, and as such can be used to authorise relatively small-scale events held in or on any premises involving fewer than 500 people at any one time, subject to certain restrictions.

Contact the environmental or licensing department of your council for details of how to apply for this.

Do note that the definition of the sale of alcohol also includes events where alcoholic drinks are included in the ticket price, or where donations are accepted in place of a fixed price.

Alcohol as raffle or tombola prizes

These are exempt as long as:

- There are no monetary prizes

- The alcohol is in sealed containers

- Tickets are only sold during the event and the raffle or tombola is drawn at the event.

- The lottery is promoted as an incident of an exempt entertainment.

- Participating in the lottery or in gaming is not the main inducement to attend the entertainment.

- Proceeds of the entertainment and raffle (after deduction of expenses) are not used for private gain.

Food standards

See the chapter on Catering for some general food safety guidelines.

More detailed information can be had from the Food Standards Agency: **www.food.gov.uk**

Food Standards Agency
Aviation House
125 Kingsway
London WC2B 6NH
Switchboard: 020 7276 8000
Emergencies only: 020 7270 8960

Public Entertainment Licences

If two or more people are going to be performing or dancing at an event that you are charging entry for, or holding to make a profit, you will need a Public Entertainment Licence. These licences cover procedures for things like noise pollution and fire hazards.

It may be that your event is taking place in a venue that already holds a licence, such as a community centre. If this is the case, you will not have to apply for a separate licence but you will have to comply with the terms of their licence.

If you do need to apply for a temporary licence for your event, you must do so at least three months in advance. Contact the licensing department of your local authority. They will tell you exactly what you need to do in order to comply with the licence regarding fire exits and similar safety measures.

What does this include?

Regulated entertainments include plays, sporting events, boxing matches, film screenings, live music and playing of recorded music.

Exemptions are:

- Entertainment or facilities for the purposes of, or incidental to, religious meetings or services or at places of public religious worship.

- Entertainment at garden fêtes, or functions or events of a similar character, provided the proceeds are not for private gain.

- Morris dancing and other dancing of a similar nature.

- Entertainment or entertainment facilities on a moving vehicle when the vehicle is not permanently or temporarily parked.

When to contact the police

The Police National Legal Database states that you must contact the police if you are holding a public procession which is intending to either:

- demonstrate support for or opposition to the views or actions of any person or body of persons.

- publicise a cause or campaign.

- mark or commemorate an event.

If you think your event may be counted as such, you should give the police advance notice of your procession, telling them the date, time and route of the procession and the name and address of the organisers, six days before the event.

If the event is not classed as a public procession then it might be still worthwhile contacting your local police station to inform them about the event.

What can our website do for you?

If you want more information about any of our books, you'll find it at **www.whiteladderpress.com**. In particular you'll find extracts from each of our books, and reviews of those that are already published. We also run special offers on future titles if you order online before publication. And you can request a copy of our free catalogue.

Many of our books also have links pages, useful addresses and so on relevant to the subject of the book. You'll also find out a bit more about us and, if you're a writer yourself, you'll find our submission guidelines for authors. So please check us out and let us know if you have any comments, questions or suggestions.

For anyone wanting to know how to launch an action group to halt some threat to a community from official madness or corporate greed, this book is the starting point. **Christopher Booker**

NOT
IN OUR
BACK
YARD

How to run a protest campaign and save the neighbourhood

So what are they trying to do? Put up a mobile phone mast near the school playing field? Build a hundred new homes on the edge of the village? Close the local hospital? Construct a wind farm on a popular beauty spot?

Fighting against local government or big bureaucracies can seem overwhelming for small communities. But in fact the odds are often better than you think.

Antony Jay, co-creator of *Yes, Minister* and *Yes, Prime Minister* and its arch bureaucrat Sir Humphrey Appleby, knows a thing or two about how to defeat bureaucracy, public or private, national or local. In *Not In Our Back Yard* he sets out the strategy you need in order to win your battle, whether you're fighting a major town bypass scheme or the closure of a small village school. Discover:

- how to organise your community into an effective force
- tactics for delaying, blocking and attacking the plan
- how to get maximum attention from the bureaucrats, the media and the local people
- how to plan and execute your campaign
- how to deal with the bureaucrats' counter-attack

This is your guide to turn indignation and outrage into effective, organised opposition.

£7.99

The OUTDOOR POCKET BIBLE

EVERY OUTDOOR RULE OF THUMB *at your fingertips*

PAUL JENNER & CHRISTINE SMITH

When you're out and about enjoying the countryside the last thing you need is to lug around several different guides to wildlife, geology, meteorology, and any other 'ology. But there are plenty of things you'd like to look up if you could. How do you light a fire when all the wood is wet? Are those fox tracks or dog tracks? Is it going to rain?

Generally there's nothing you can do but hope for the best, or maybe phone a friend if you can get reception, and they're in, and they know the answer…

That's where this book is so brilliant. It has the answers to more questions than you'd think could fit into such a handy volume. You'll find out pretty much anything you need to know:

- ◆ Emergency advice, from basic first aid to how to escape from quicksand
- ◆ Help with navigation, such as telling which way is north by your watch, or by the moon
- ◆ Identification guides: constellations, seashells and shore life, semi-precious stones, burial mounds, animal tracks and more
- ◆ Boating guidelines, from tides to tying knots to what the buoys mean
- ◆ Which wild food you can eat and how to recognise it
- ◆ Weather lore, such as which clouds indicate what kind of weather

This is the only book you really can't do without when you're out and about. So you can ditch that library of guidebooks and slip this in your pocket instead.

Price £7.99

Index

Useful contacts

You'll find all the websites referred to in this book on our website at **www.whiteladderpress.com** to make it easier for you to access them. Click on 'Useful contacts' next to the information about this book.

Contact us

You're welcome to contact White Ladder Press if you have any questions or comments for either us or the author. Please use whichever of the following routes suits you.

Phone 01803 813343 between 9am and 5.30pm

Email enquiries@whiteladderpress.com

Fax 01803 813928

Address White Ladder Press, Great Ambrook, Near Ipplepen, Devon TQ12 5UL

Website www.whiteladderpress.com

Conclusion

The best fundraising ideas are the ideas that come from the heart. Think big, think bold, and go for broke! And try to enjoy yourself. You'll raise more cash, enthuse more people and get more out of it yourself if you choose something you will have fun doing.

Be inspired by some of the stories of successful fundraisers within this book, and spend plenty of time getting things nailed down at the ideas stage. As you've read many times, research and planning really are key to the success of your efforts, so make sure you put the groundwork in here and you'll reap the rewards later. Make sure everyone knows what they're doing and when their tasks need to be done by. Keep careful records and, even more importantly, watch your bottom line.

Use every friend, family member, colleague and co-worker. Exploit all your contacts and work every possible avenue. Use the internet. Write to celebrities and businesses. Get the media interested. Write a great press release.

And if you do all this, with a bit of luck, a splash of inspiration and a lot of hard work, your small group can raise big funds.

Good luck!